One Salvation, Three Stages

Be Saved, Being Saved, and Shall Be Saved

One Salvation, Three Stages

Be Saved, Being Saved, and Shall Be Saved

Vinu V Das

Tabor Press

ISBN 978-1-997541-24-0

Table of Contents

Chapter 1. Framing the Three-Tense Gospel

Salvation is the most familiar word in Christian vocabulary and yet one of the most profoundly misunderstood. New believers frequently reduce it to the moment they "asked Jesus into their heart." Seasoned saints, wary of legalism, sometimes equate it exclusively with the lifelong journey of discipleship. Eschatologically minded Christians press every hope into the future day when Christ will appear and transform our lowly bodies. Scripture, however, insists that the gospel is simultaneously past, present, and future: we **have been saved** (completed act), we **are being saved** (continuing process), and we **shall be saved** (promised consummation). If the church is to proclaim a full-orbed message that liberates the sinner, stabilizes the pilgrim, and emboldens the expectant bride, it must recover the grammar, scope, and hermeneutics of a three-tensed gospel. This opening chapter therefore supplies the linguistic scaffolding, methodological commitments, and interpretive guardrails that undergird every later discussion in this volume. The reader is invited to linger here; mastery of these foundations will sharpen discernment throughout the remaining chapters and prevent the drift into reductionism so common in contemporary soteriological debates.

1.1 The Grammar of Salvation

The first task is grammatical, not in the trivial sense of parsing sentences but in the weightier sense of noticing how inspired authors use time-referencing verbs and nouns to describe God's saving work. Language is never ornamental in the Bible; it is revelation's chosen vessel. Accordingly, each of the three subsections below traces verbal tenses, analyzes core salvation terms in their original languages, and then shows how Christ gathers the temporal strands into a single, coherent tapestry.

1.1.1 Verb Tenses in Scripture

The apostle Paul, a master logician and seasoned pastor, employs deliberate tenses when writing about salvation. In **Ephesians 2:5** he asserts, "by grace you *have been saved*," employing the perfect tense to emphasize a completed reality with abiding results. Conversely, in **1 Corinthians 1:18** he states that "the word of the cross...is the power of God to *those who are being saved*," using a present participle that stresses ongoing action. Later, in **Romans 13:11**, he exhorts believers to awake because "now is our salvation *nearer* than when we believed," harkening forward to an eschatological horizon. These textual observations are not pedantic; they guard against theological myopia. When the perfect tense is flattened into a mere hope, assurance evaporates. When the present participle is ignored, discipleship decays into passive presumption. When the future aspect is jettisoned, Christian hope collapses into this-world activism. Each tense therefore functions as a theological checkpoint.

Yet these grammatical distinctions are not isolated to Paul. **Hebrews 10:10, 14** juxtaposes a perfect "we have been sanctified" with a present "are being perfected," and **1 Peter 1:5** intertwines believers who "are being guarded" for a salvation "ready to be revealed." The inspired writers consistently hold the three dimensions in creative tension, demonstrating that grammar is gospel architecture. Ten sentences cannot exhaust the multi-layered artistry, but they can alert the reader to observe verbs with reverent precision. Every subsequent doctrine—justification, sanctification, glorification—rests on this textual bedrock.

1.1.2 Soteriological Terms in Hebrew and Greek

While English Bibles uniformly render many words as *save* or *salvation*, the underlying languages carry rich connotations that color each tense. The Hebrew verb יָשַׁע (*yasha*) evokes deliverance from danger, whether military (Exod 14:30) or existential (Ps 34:6). It can describe a decisive rescue event— Israel crossing the Red Sea—yet prophetic literature often uses participial forms to reveal an ongoing posture, as in Isaiah's portrait of God as the continually "saving" Rock. The noun יְשׁוּעָה (*yeshuʿah*) not only names the act but also the space of well-being that results. This dual nuance foreshadows Israel's experience: saved *from* Egypt, being saved *through* the wilderness, and awaiting salvation *into* the land of rest.

Greek amplifies the spectrum. Σῴζω (*sōzō*), the principal verb in the New Testament, retains the Hebrew sense of rescue but overlays it with spiritual redemption (Matt 1:21) and physical healing (Mark 5:34). Its cognate noun σωτηρία (*sōtēria*) spans emancipation from sin's penalty (Acts 4:12) to the final unveiling of glory (Heb 9:28). The present participial construction τοῖς σῳζομένοις in 1 Corinthians 1:18 signals continuous action, while the future passive σωθήσῃ in Romans 10:9 promises consummation. Lexical study therefore cautions against restricting salvation vocabulary to a single time slice; the semantic field itself is fluid, traversing moments, journeys, and destinies.

By tracing Hebrew and Greek usage across canon-wide contexts—narrative, poetry, prophecy, epistle—one discovers

13

that soteriological lexemes are inherently elastic. They flex to describe punctual deliverance (Noah stepping out of the ark), progressive liberation (Israel shedding Egypt's mindset), and eschatological completion (the New Jerusalem). Word studies thus join grammar to confirm that salvation is a story told in three tenses.

1.1.3 Uniting the Tenses in Christ

Having considered verbs and vocabulary, we now ask the integrating question: *Who* unites the tenses? The answer is not merely a doctrinal formula but a Person—Jesus Christ. The Johannine title "I AM" (John 8:58) already collapses past, present, and future into divine immediacy. At the cross He accomplished redemption once for all (John 19:30), yet by His resurrection He lives to intercede, actively mediating present grace (Heb 7:25), and by His promised return He pledges universal restoration (Rev 21:5). Christ Himself is therefore the hermeneutical key; He is the alpha of completed salvation, the ongoing omega of transformative saving, and the eschatological horizon toward which every redeemed life points.

Paul's famous triad in **1 Thessalonians 5:23**—"may your spirit and soul and body be kept *blameless* at the coming of our Lord Jesus Christ"—shows how Christ's parousia circles back to safeguard the believer's present sanctification, which is grounded in His past atonement. Likewise, **Titus 2:11–13** anchors ethical instruction in the appearing of grace (past), the training of grace (present), and the blessed hope (future). In Christ time bends; history, daily obedience, and destiny all meet in Him. Uniting the tenses in Christ protects the church from fragmenting into competing schools: the forensic camp (past), the spiritual-formation camp (present), and the eschatological speculation camp (future). A Christocentric grammar prevents partial gospels. Consequently, every chapter that follows will consciously tether its assertions to the living Christ who spans eternity and invades every temporal dimension with redemptive purpose.

1.2 Purpose and Scope of This Book

If Section 1.1 answered *what* the three-tensed gospel is, Section 1.2 answers *why* this book exists, *how* it approaches the subject, and *where* the reader is going. Clarity here forestalls disappointment later.

1.2.1 Why Another Book on Salvation?

At first glance the market appears saturated with volumes on soteriology, ranging from scholarly tomes to devotional pamphlets. Yet many influential works privilege one tense at the expense of the others. Popular evangelistic literature glories in justification but says little about sanctification's rigor or glorification's hope. Spiritual-formation classics immerse readers in present disciplines yet treat past pardon as assumed and future glory as hazy. Prophetic texts fire the imagination with celestial vistas but sometimes neglect the ethical imperatives of daily cross-bearing. This fragmentation breeds malnourished disciples—converted but restless, diligent but insecure, hopeful but escapist. By re-braiding the tenses into a single cord, this book aims to nourish the whole person.

The need is pastoral as well as theological. Counseling rooms echo with questions that betray confusion: "If I sinned grievously yesterday, was I ever truly saved?" "Why pursue holiness if I'm already secure?" "Does the tribulation timeline affect my everyday walk?" These are not academic puzzles; they shape assurance, obedience, and mission. A volume that patiently unfolds the grammar, process, and promise of salvation can stabilize wobbling hearts. For these reasons—doctrinal balance and pastoral urgency—another book is justified.

1.2.2 Methodology and Theological Lens

Methodologically, the book adopts a canonical-biblical theology framework. Rather than extracting proof texts, it follows salvation's progressive revelation from Eden to the

New Jerusalem, letting each epoch contribute its distinctive witness. Typology is employed judiciously: Israel's exodus, for instance, is treated as both historical deliverance and prototype of spiritual liberation (1 Cor 10:1–4). Systematic categories—justification, regeneration, adoption—are acknowledged but arranged chronologically to preserve narrative flow.

The primary theological lens is Christocentric and Trinitarian. The Father plans, the Son accomplishes, and the Spirit applies salvation, yet the divine unity prevents dissecting grace into detachable parts. Reformed soteriology heavily influences the exposition of monergistic regeneration and forensic justification, while Wesleyan and Eastern emphases on participatory holiness enrich discussions of sanctification. This irenic posture seeks to honor the breadth of the Christian tradition without muting essential distinctions. Critical engagement with contemporary debates—such as the New Perspective on Paul and the "Free Grace" controversy—will appear in later chapters, but always in service of clarifying rather than polarizing.

1.2.3 Reader's Roadmap

Because salvation's scope is vast, readers require a map. Chapter 1 (the present chapter) erects the conceptual scaffolding. Chapters 2–4 will explore the necessity, foundation, and decisive moment of being "saved once," focusing on the crisis of justification and new birth. Chapters 5–9 will trace the lifelong pilgrimage of "being saved," examining sanctification, Spirit-empowered living, community dynamics, and perseverance. Chapters 10–11 will lift the gaze to the climactic "shall be saved," surveying resurrection, judgment seat rewards, and new-creation hope, before folding those vistas back into present ethics. Chapter 12 will summarize and exhort. Appendices will address disputed passages and offer study guides for small groups.

Readers may progress linearly or consult sections as needs arise, but each chapter is crafted to stand alone while contributing to the cumulative argument. Sidebars provide word-study nuggets, church-history anecdotes, and contemporary applications. Reflection questions close every chapter, nudging readers from comprehension to transformation. The roadmap is not merely logistical; it mirrors the three-tensed gospel itself: orientation (past rescue), pilgrimage (present journey), and destination (future glory).

1.3 Key Hermeneutical Principles

A book that mishandles Scripture will inevitably misrepresent salvation. Therefore, before exploring doctrines, we must establish interpretive principles that safeguard fidelity.

1.3.1 Scripture Interprets Scripture

The Protestant Reformers' axiom *scriptura sui ipsius interpres* (Scripture is its own interpreter) protects against eisegesis, the reading of foreign ideas into the text. When encountering a difficult verse—such as **Philippians 2:12**, "work out your own salvation"—one must consult clearer passages on justification by grace through faith (Eph 2:8–9) to prevent works-righteousness. Conversely, reassuring texts like **John 10:28–29** on eternal security must be held alongside warnings such as **Hebrews 6:4–6** to avoid antinomian laxity. The canon's diverse voices harmonize when each is allowed to speak on its own terms and then weighed together.

Practically, this means cross-referencing themes, tracing intertextual allusions, and honoring covenantal trajectories. When Paul calls the Exodus generation "baptized into Moses" (1 Cor 10:2), he invites readers to view Christian baptism through an Old-Testament salvation lens. Such canonical resonance deepens rather than diminishes meaning. Thus, interpretive rigor is an act of worship, acknowledging the Spirit's unifying authorship across time.

1.3.2 Historical-Grammatical Controls

While spiritualizing tendencies can yield edifying applications, they risk severing text from context. The historical-grammatical method insists that meaning resides first in what the original author intended and original audience understood. Therefore, study of genre, syntax, and cultural setting is indispensable. **Jeremiah 29:11**, often quoted as a blank-check promise, originally addressed exiles facing seventy years of discipline. Appreciating that background tempers triumphal interpretations and situates the verse within a salvation narrative that includes judgment, exile, and eventual restoration—a pattern mirrored in personal conversion stories.

Grammar also guards against anachronism. For instance, the future-oriented **1 Peter 1:5** "ready to be revealed" employs an aorist participle that looks forward, not backward; reading it as present possession obscures Petrine eschatology. Moreover, knowledge of second-temple Jewish expectations illuminates phrases like "kingdom of heaven," safeguarding against purely spiritualized readings that ignore tangible new-creation hope. In short, historical-grammatical controls tether theological imagination to inspired intent.

1.3.3 Christological Center

Finally, all Scripture must be read in light of Christ (Luke 24:27). This does not mean forcing allegories onto every minor detail but recognizing that covenants, types, and promises converge in Him. For salvation studies, the Christological lens prevents detaching benefits from Benefactor. Justification is not an abstract verdict; it is union with the crucified-and-risen Lord (Rom 6:5). Sanctification is not moral polishing; it is Christ formed in us (Gal 4:19). Glorification is not ethereal bliss; it is being "conformed to the image of His Son" (Rom 8:29).

Christ's mediatorial offices—Prophet, Priest, King—also align with the three tenses: prophetic word awakens past faith (Acts 3:22–23), priestly intercession sustains present pilgrimage (Heb 7:25), and kingly return secures future victory (Rev 19:11–16). Therefore, exegesis that sidelines Christ, however sophisticated, will invariably skew salvation. By contrast, Christ-centered hermeneutics illuminate the unity of Scripture and fuel doxology.

Conclusion

This opening chapter has erected the scaffolding for everything to come: grammatical observations safeguard the three tenses; lexical studies broaden semantic horizons; Christ unites temporal strands; methodological clarity explains why and how the book proceeds; hermeneutical principles anchor interpretation. Readers now possess the tools to explore each phase of salvation without collapsing them into one or tearing them apart. The journey ahead will move from the necessity of rescue to the glory of consummation, but the grammar, purpose, and interpretive commitments forged here will remain our compass. May the Holy Spirit, who inspired the text and orchestrates every dimension of redemption, grant understanding as we travel through the unfolding splendor of being saved, being saved still, and waiting to be saved utterly.

Chapter 2. Why We Must Be Saved

Every human life unfolds against an inescapable backdrop: beings created to reflect divine glory yet born into a world broken by rebellion. From our first breath, we inherit a legacy of corrupted hearts, fractured relationships, and a cosmos groaning under futility. The Bible does not shy away from this stark reality—in its pages we confront the ruin that marred Eden's original design and recognize how every human endeavor at moral improvement falls short of God's unyielding standard. Scripture describes our plight in vivid terms: spiritual death that severs our fellowship with the Source of life (Eph 2:1), legal condemnation that pronounces guilt upon every person (Rom 3:23), and an inherited corruption so deep that even our noblest impulses bear the taint of selfishness (Jer 17:9). Yet these diagnoses are not offered as exercises in despair but as indispensable prelude to hope. By laying bare the depth and breadth of sin's devastation—legal, moral, relational, cosmic, and eternal—the divine narrative exposes the futility of self-salvation and the impossibility of meeting God's justice through human effort. This chapter opens our eyes to why the human condition demands a rescue that originates beyond ourselves, preparing us to receive the grace that alone can restore what sin has shattered.

2.1 Creation's Original Design

2.1.1 Bearing God's image—vice-regency on earth

Human beings alone among the creatures are described as made "in the image of God," a unique designation that sets humanity apart with dignity and purpose (Gen 1:26–28). This divine imprint means that people reflect God's character, moral capacity, and relational nature, carrying within them a spark of the Creator's own identity. As image-bearers, humans were commissioned to exercise delegated authority over the rest of creation, stewarding ecosystems, naming animals, and exercising wise dominion. Such vice-regency was not exploitative but custodial, involving benevolent oversight that mirrored God's care for the cosmos. Furthermore, bearing God's image endowed humans with intrinsic worth, meaning that every life—from the first couple to every descendant—possesses sacred value irrespective of status or ability. This foundational truth underscores why the destruction of human life or dignity is especially grievous in God's sight. In addition, image-bearing entails moral capacity: Adam and Eve were created with freedom to choose, to love, and to obey, reflecting the relational dimension of the Trinity. Their choices would therefore have real significance, not mere illusion, since they were made in God's likeness. Moreover, the image of God anticipated a covenantal partnership: humanity's obedience and stewardship were designed to participate in God's plan for earth's flourishing. Tragically, as we shall later see, the fall marred that image, but the original design remains the measure of what salvation intends to restore. By anchoring identity in divine imprint, Scripture establishes both our greatness in creation and the depth of our ruin when that image is tarnished.

2.1.2 Moral innocence & relational harmony

At the dawn of creation, Adam and Eve lived in a state of moral innocence, unburdened by guilt or shame (Gen 2:25). Their hearts were free from deceit, envy, or malice, because corruption had not yet entered their natures. In this pristine condition, every choice was marked by spontaneity in obedience and delight in God's commands. Moreover, innocence fostered harmonious relationship between the man and the woman; they communed openly, unashamed of nakedness or hidden motives. This harmony extended upward—walking with God in the cool of the day—reflecting fellowship unspoiled by fear or alienation (Gen 3:8). It also extended horizontally between humanity and creation, as animals and the land itself submitted without hostility to human stewardship. The moral equilibrium of Eden meant that there was no compulsion or inner struggle to obey God; delight and duty were inseparable, rooted in the joy of a flawless nature. In addition, relational harmony included the communal dimension: Adam named the beasts, yet always longed for a covenantal companion, until Eve was created as "bone of his bones" (Gen 2:23). The seamless unity between husband and wife exemplified God's intention for human community. Thus, moral innocence and relational harmony formed the bedrock of human flourishing, a pattern shattered by the fall and therefore the very condition salvation seeks to reestablish.

2.1.3 Worshipful work—cultivating and guarding Eden

Work was instituted not as curse but as worshipful vocation in Eden (Gen 2:15). In the Garden, Adam was appointed to "dress and keep" the land, a dual role combining creativity and custody. Cultivation involved cultivating crops, nurturing trees, and stewarding biodiversity, demonstrating God's image through fruitful labor. Guarding signified protection—warding off threats from wild beasts or decay—symbolizing the priestly task of safeguarding holiness. Far from burdensome toil, this labor was infused with communion; while working the soil, Adam conversed with God, learning divine truths even as he tilled the ground. This synergy of work and worship established the sacredness of everyday activity, foreshadowing how redeemed believers would integrate faith and profession. Moreover, Eden's horticultural paradise reflected the promise of new creation, where righteousness and peace would flourish unchecked. The rhythms of sowing and resting in Eden anticipated Sabbath patterns, embedding worship into time itself. Thus, the original human vocation combined mind, body, and spirit in glorifying God through fruitful stewardship—a vision tragically derailed by sin but destined for restoration in Christ.

While Eden's design revealed humanity at its best—image-bearing, innocent, and joyfully at work—the next section traces how that ideal was shattered in a single fateful moment, plunging creation into chaos and exposing our deep need for rescue.

2.2 The Catastrophe of the Fall

2.2.1 The serpent's deception & human rebellion

In the Garden, the tempter appeared not as a roaring beast but as a cunning serpent, subverting Eden's harmony through half-truths and insinuations (Gen 3:1–3). By questioning God's command—"Did God really say…?"—the serpent planted seeds of doubt about divine goodness and wisdom. Eve's response, omitting part of the prohibition, opened the door to further distortion: the creature's lies capitalized on partial truths to mislead her heart. When the serpent promised that eating the forbidden fruit would make them "like God," Eve's ambition for autonomy overcame her trust in God's loving authority. Adam, standing alongside her, joined in the rebellion, choosing solidarity with Eve over solidarity with God. Their united act of disobedience represented not merely an ethical lapse but cosmic treason, as vice-regents turned against their Sovereign. The fruit itself, once a gift of sustenance, became the instrument of spiritual death. What began as a matter of curiosity became the catalyst for universal corruption. Thus the fall was no minor mistake; it was a deliberate betrayal that severed humanity's reliance on God and ushered in shame, fear, and chaos.

2.2.2 Broken fellowship—hiding from God

The immediate aftermath of that rebellion was not a hail of lightning or a crushing earthquake but the subtle pang of shame and the impulse to hide (Gen 3:7–8). Nakedness, once a symbol of vulnerability embraced in innocence, became reason for covering and concealment. When God walked in the Garden's cool breeze, He called, "Where are you?"—a question that pierced their guilty hearts. Rather than stand in the convicting presence of their Creator, Adam and Eve retreated behind fig leaves and seclusion among the trees. This flight illustrated how sin's first fruit is relational rupture: shame drives us away from intimacy rather than toward confession. Hiding from God marked humanity's new default posture—concealment instead of communion. Even in modern times, spiritual shame prompts many to avoid prayer, skip worship, or cover sins instead of bringing them into the light. The primal act of hiding foretells the ultimate need for restoration of fellowship, a need that only divine grace can meet.

2.2.3 Curses on vocation, relationships, and creation

God's response to the fall was not vindictive but judicial: He pronounced curses that revealed sin's consequences across every dimension of life (Gen 3:16–19). To the woman He declared multiplied pain in childbirth and relational tension with her husband, introducing strife into the most intimate human bond. To the man He assigned "cursed ground," transforming his once-delightful labor into painful toil, marked by thorns and sweat. These curses were not arbitrary punishments but realistic prognoses of how disobedience fissions the fabric of existence. Where work had been worshipful, it would now be wearisome; where relationship had been loving, it would bear conflict; and where creation had been benign, it would grow hostile. Theology later interprets these curses as emblematic of the world's fallen state, where injustice, disease, and death attest to brokenness. The voice that once blessed life now declared hardship, reminding humanity that sin's aftershocks ripple far beyond a personal misstep.

2.2.4 Exile as symbol of separation

Finally, having uprooted their innocence and banished Eden's peace, God expelled Adam and Eve from the garden (Gen 3:23–24). Exile signified loss of access to life's source—Eden's tree of life—and foreshadowed the spiritual death that accompanies separation from God. The cherubim and flaming sword guarding the entrance illustrated divine holiness that cannot abide sin. Exile became the archetype for every subsequent human estrangement: nations exiled from their homelands, individuals exiled from God's presence by obstinate rebellion. Spiritual exile defines the plight of every person who ever lived outside of Christ. Only a return from exile—through divine provision—can restore the relationship broken by the fall.

The fall's catastrophe unleashed not only relational rupture and exile but also ushered in a fourfold corruption that permeates every aspect of human existence. Section 2.3 now examines how sin's stain extends into guilt, pollution, alienation, and cosmic disorder.

2.3 Sin's Fourfold Corruption

2.3.1 Legal guilt—standing condemned

Sin's first consequence is legal guilt: humanity stands condemned before a holy God whose law has been transgressed. Scripture declares, "None is righteous, no, not one," indicting every human heart without exception (Rom 3:10–12). This condemnation is forensic, akin to a courtroom verdict, and leaves the sinner liable to just penalty. The law functions as a mirror, exposing hidden transgressions rather than offering remedy (Rom 7:7). In this state, no amount of moral striving can erase the record of guilt; every good deed is tainted by sin's presence (Isa 64:6). The awareness of legal liability generates fear rather than confidence, compelling many to either harden their hearts or despair entirely. Until guilt is addressed, humanity cannot enter into fellowship with God, for justice demands satisfaction of divine law. Thus, the doctrine of guilt highlights why mere moral improvement is insufficient; only divine intervention can satisfy the demands of justice.

2.3.2 Moral pollution—darkened mind and heart

Beyond guilt, sin entails moral pollution: a defilement of the inner person that distorts understanding and perverts desires (Jer 17:9). The heart becomes a breeding ground for deceit, lust, envy, and pride, twisting the moral compass and leading to progressively darker choices. Scripture warns that the mind "becomes futile" and "darkened in its understanding" apart from God's renewing work (Eph 4:17–18). Moral pollution thus is not a superficial stain but a deep corruption that infects thought patterns, speech, and motivations. It blinds individuals to spiritual realities, making the wisdom of God seem foolish and suppressing the truth (Rom 1:21–22). As hearts grow hardened, they resist conviction and reread God's law through a lens of self-justification. This internal decay undergirds every visible act of wrongdoing and further emphasizes humanity's need for cleansing that transcends self-help.

2.3.3 Relational alienation—from God and neighbor

The fall fractured not only the individual but also relationships—both vertical and horizontal. Sin erects barriers between humanity and God, cutting off the flow of love, peace, and guidance. Scripture tells us that "your iniquities have made a separation between you and your God" (Isa 59:2), portraying sin as a chasm that only divine bridge-building can span. Horizontally, alienation manifests in broken families, fractured communities, and social injustices—envy breeding conflict (Jas 4:1), pride leading to oppression, and selfishness corroding empathy. Sin turns neighbor into rival, eroding sympathy and fostering exploitation. Thus relational alienation reflects moral pollution gone public, and without reconciliation, both personal and social harmony remain elusive.

2.3.4 Cosmic disorder—creation subjected to futility

Finally, sin's effects extend into the created order, subjecting the heavens and earth to disorder and decay. Paul personifies creation groaning under futility, waiting for liberation from corruption (Rom 8:20–22). Natural disasters, disease, and ecological breakdown all bear witness to the curse pronounced in Genesis. The once-harmonious interplay of elements now exhibits tension: earthquakes shake the ground, storms ravage coasts, and organisms compete rather than coexist peacefully. This cosmic disorder reminds us that sin is not merely a personal issue but a structural one, affecting every realm under heaven. The hope of redemption thus encompasses not only souls but the very fabric of creation itself.

Having surveyed sin's legal, moral, relational, and cosmic ravages, we turn next to human inability—our incapacity to reverse these effects by our own efforts—and why only God-initiated salvation can overcome such entrenched corruption.

2.4 Human Inability

2.4.1 Bondage of the will—unable to seek God

Even after the fall, humans often believe that salvation is merely a matter of human choice and willpower. Scripture, however, reveals that the will is in bondage to sin, unable to initiate genuine seeking of God apart from divine grace (John 6:44). Like captives in chains, unregenerate minds remain hostile toward the things of God, viewing God's commands as burdensome rather than beautiful (Rom 8:7–8). The bondage of the will explains why folk wisdom—"just decide to do better"—fails spectacularly in transforming lives. Those bound by sin lack the ability to choose God because their affections and intellect are ensnared by corruption. Only when God regenerates the heart does the will find freedom to pursue righteousness and truth. Regeneration precedes and enables genuine response; without it, sincerity cannot overcome the entrenched habits of sin. This theological truth underscores the necessity of monergistic grace in salvation.

2.4.2 Powerlessness against death

Death is the unavoidable consequence of sin, and the human condition is characterized by a fundamental powerlessness to evade it. Hebrews teaches that Christ partook of flesh and blood "so that through death He might destroy the one who has the power of death, that is, the devil" (Heb 2:14). Humanity's mortality—physical, spiritual, and ultimately eternal separation—is not a condition we can reverse on our own. Medical advances may prolong life, but they cannot guarantee freedom from decay or the second death (Rev 20:14). The universal experience of loss and grief attests to death's reign over every family and culture. In this powerless state, humans cry out for hope, but any attempt to conquer death through human ingenuity inevitably fails. Only the divine Conqueror of death, Christ Himself, can impart the life-giving Spirit that breaks death's dominion and secures eternal life.

2.4.3 Futility of self-salvation projects—religion, morality, philosophy

Throughout history, humanity has turned to religion, moral reform, and philosophical systems in an effort to find meaning and escape from sin's penalty. Yet every such project falters because it assumes the very thing that is missing: a heart susceptible to God's influence. Ritual observances become empty without genuine inner transformation (Col 2:23), moral codes become burdensome legalism without the power to fulfill them, and philosophical systems end in existential despair when confronted by oblivion. Even the most rigorous ethical philosophies lack the authority to remake desires or remove guilt. These self-salvation endeavors highlight human pride: the belief that we can save ourselves by our own resources. Scripture challenges this presumption by presenting a righteousness that is utterly foreign to self-effort—"the righteousness of God through faith" (Rom 3:22). Only divine rescue can deliver humanity from the futility of its own delusions of self-sufficiency.

Having seen both the depth of sin's devastation and human inability to resolve it, we will next explore God's holiness and justice—the divine response that makes salvation not only necessary but also radically gracious.

2.5 Divine Holiness and Justice

2.5.1 God's moral perfection—"eyes too pure to look on evil"

God's holiness is the ground of His entire moral character, a perfection so absolute that evil cannot exist in His presence even momentarily. When the prophet Habakkuk declares that God's eyes are "too pure to look on evil," he underscores the utter separation between divine purity and human sinfulness (Hab 1:13). This moral perfection is not merely an absence of wrongdoing but an active, radiant excellence that repels every shadow of darkness. Every divine decree issues from this flawless essence, ensuring that God's actions are never capricious or unjust. His will reflects a harmony of love and righteousness, such that what He commands is inherently good and life-giving. In contrast, humanity's sense of morality wavers with culture and circumstance; by contrast, God's standard does not shift with the wind. Because God is unchanging (Mal 3:6), His holy standard stands immutable across every generation. This immutable holiness means He must oppose evil at its core, not merely punish it as a peripheral misdemeanor. The doctrine of God's perfect purity thus reveals why no sinner can stand in His presence unmediated: our transgressions are too offensive to escape His righteous notice. The tension between divine holiness and human sin creates the very context in which salvation must occur—God cannot ignore sin without compromising His essence. Understanding God's moral perfection is therefore the prerequisite for grasping both His justice and His mercy.

2.5.2 Wrath as settled opposition to sin

God's wrath is sometimes misunderstood as capricious anger, yet Scripture presents it as His settled, essential opposition to sin's destructive power (Rom 1:18). This wrath is not a loss of self-control but a steady, determined stance against anything that mars His perfect creation. Just as a loving parent reacts firmly against anything that endangers a child, God's wrath functions to uphold moral order and purge corruption. Divine displeasure is proportional to the gravity of sin, reflecting His intimate knowledge of every hidden motive and deed. The cross itself testifies to the fierce reality of God's wrath: Christ endured the cup of God's righteous indignation so that believers would never taste its full consequence. Yet this wrath is not untempered; it operates within the framework of divine love, a love so profound that the Son would suffer in our place (Isa 53:10). Thus, God's wrath is both an expression of His justice and a component of His redemptive strategy. Without an appreciation for the depth of God's hostility to sin, we cannot understand the magnitude of what Christ accomplished. Wrath underscores the chasm that stood between a holy God and fallen humanity and sets the stage for the astonishing grace that bridges that chasm.

2.5.3 The necessity of just retribution

In tandem with His holiness and wrath, God's justice requires that every infraction against His law receive appropriate retribution. This is not vengeance in the human sense but a lawful balancing of moral accounts, ensuring that wrongdoing does not go unaddressed. The Old Testament law with its sacrificial system illustrated this principle vividly: every sin demanded a corresponding offering, symbolizing the seriousness of violating covenantal standards (Lev 5:17–19). Retribution establishes the credibility of divine norms; without it, God's commands would ring hollow. The principle of "a life for a life" (Num 35:31) echoes in the New Testament affirmation that Christ bore the penalty due to sinners, satisfying divine justice on their behalf (2 Cor 5:21). Retribution thus becomes a means whereby justice and mercy intersect: the requirement for punishment is met, yet the guilty are spared because Christ endures the sentence. If just retribution were optional, law and love would be in conflict; the cross shows how they converge. Therefore, any notion of cheap grace that neglects God's need for retribution distorts the gospel. It is precisely because retribution is necessary that salvation must be both costly and divine in origin.

2.5.4 Tension with divine love—setting the stage for redemption

God's justice and wrath exist in dynamic tension with His immutable love. The familiar declaration in Exodus that God is "merciful and gracious, slow to anger, abounding in steadfast love" (Ex 34:6) captures this interplay. Divine love does not negate justice but informs how justice is executed—through sacrificial substitution rather than mere destruction. In the garden of Eden, God's judgment fell on the serpent, yet hope emerged immediately in the promise of a Seed who would crush evil's head. This proto-evangelium reveals that divine love anticipates and addresses the consequences of sin without compromising holiness. Love motivates God to provide a remedy, to send the Son into the world so that condemned sinners might become beloved children (John 3:16; Gal 4:5–7). In this dramatic pericope, we glimpse the marriage of justice and mercy: the guilty are pardoned, yet the penalty for sin is still honored. The tension between God's love and holiness thus becomes the very ground from which redemption springs. Without embracing this tension, one risks envisioning a sentimental deity indifferent to moral order or a harsh judge devoid of compassion. The Christian narrative resolves this tension decisively in the person and work of Christ, setting the stage for salvation's necessity and sufficiency.

While Section 2.5 surveyed God's character—His holiness, wrath, justice, and love—Section 2.6 turns to the manifold consequences that sin unleashes, consequences that God's justice demands must be addressed by divine intervention.

2.6 Comprehensive Consequences of Sin

2.6.1 Spiritual death—separation from the Source of life

Sin's most immediate consequence is spiritual death: an irreversible break between the human soul and its Creator. Scripture portrays this as darkness enveloping the person, where once there was communion and light (Eph 2:1). This separation is not symbolic but existential: without the

31

animating presence of God, the soul cannot experience true life. Just as cutting the cord halts a newborn's life, sin cuts off humanity from its life-giver. The psalmist's cry, "Cast me not away from Thy presence," echoes universal awareness of this dire state (Ps 51:11). Spiritually dead people may be physically alive and socially active, yet they are incapable of spiritual vitality, truth, or righteousness. In this state, practices that involve God—prayer, worship, service—become duties devoid of transforming power. Spiritual death also ushers in moral apathy and desensitization to evil; without God's life in the soul, the conscience grows dull. Understanding spiritual death clarifies why mere moral reform cannot suffice—only the divine act of regeneration can reverse this fatal state.

2.6.2 Physical decay and mortality

While spiritual death is primary, sin's curse extends to the physical realm, inflicting decay, disease, and ultimately bodily death. From the moment of the fall, the created order itself began to groan under corruption (Rom 8:22). The human body, once impervious to sickness or aging, now succumbs to entropy, mirroring the soul's foothold in sin. Ancient burial practices and modern cemeteries alike testify to the universal reality of mortality. "Dust thou art, and to dust thou shalt return" became the stark epitaph for every generation (Gen 3:19). Physical decay reminds us that salvation involves not only forgiveness but also restoration: the promise of resurrection life anticipates bodies free from corruption (1 Cor 15:52–54). The link between spiritual and physical death underscores the holistic nature of redemption—God intends to redeem every dimension marred by sin.

2.6.3 Eternal judgment—second death and exclusion

Beyond temporal death, Scripture warns of an eternal consequence for unrepentant sin: the second death, or exclusion from God's presence forever (Rev 20:14–15). This terrifying prospect is not a mere doctrinal abstraction but a reality depicted in vivid imagery throughout the New Testament. Jesus Himself spoke of weeping and gnashing of teeth, images that convey unending sorrow and regret (Matt

8:12). The final judgment sifts humanity, separating those who entered life through faith from those who refused grace. Unlike physical death, which all share, eternal judgment distinguishes based on response to God's revealed mercy. The doctrine of the second death highlights the urgency of the gospel message: to miss salvation is to forfeit not only temporal joys but everlasting communion with the Source of love. The reality of eternal judgment intensifies the necessity of salvation—it is not optional but imperative.

2.6.4 Societal collapse—injustice, violence, idolatry

Sin's ramifications ripple beyond individuals to societies and civilizations, producing systemic injustices, pervasive violence, and idolatrous cultural patterns. The pre-flood world offers a stark portrait: "The earth was corrupt before God, and the earth was filled with violence" (Gen 6:11). Wherever human hearts turn from God, they erect idols—whether statues, ideologies, or ambitions—and erect systems that exploit the vulnerable. Empires rise on conquest, trade networks flourish at the cost of ethical compromise, and cultural achievements mask profound moral decay. The writings of the prophets critique such societal corruption relentlessly, calling nations back to covenant faithfulness. Paul's epistle to the Romans catalogs behaviors that result from suppressing the truth, culminating in communities marked by chaos and moral collapse (Rom 1:28–32). This tragic sociological dimension of sin emphasizes that salvation must address not only personal sins but also break the power of evil in public life. It underlines the Christian calling to engage culture with redemptive hope, offering both forgiveness and transformation.

Having surveyed sin's spiritual, physical, eternal, and societal consequences, we now recognize that the need for salvation spans the entire human condition and every corner of creation. Section 2.7 will demonstrate that this desperate need is truly universal—no one is exempt from the fall's effects.

2.7 The Universal Scope of the Need

2.7.1 "No one righteous"—Jew and Gentile alike

The apostle Paul clinches the argument for humanity's universal need by quoting multiple Old Testament passages to assert that "no one is righteous, no, not one" (Rom 3:10). This sweeping indictment crosses cultural and ethnic boundaries: whether Jew or Gentile, every person's moral record falls short of God's perfect standard. Claims of moral superiority, be they religious credentials or philosophical ideals, cannot withstand this divine audit. This universality of sin prevents any group from claiming a privileged status before God. Even self-proclaimed paragons of virtue share in humanity's collective guilt, because sin is not merely a series of bad actions but a pervasive condition of the heart. Recognizing universal sinfulness lays the groundwork for understanding why salvation must be offered freely to all without partiality.

2.7.2 Corporate solidarity in Adam

Scripture portrays the entire human race as federally represented by Adam in his original act of rebellion. When Adam fell, all his descendants participated in that fall, inheriting a sinful nature and the liability of guilt (1 Cor 15:22a). This doctrine of federal headship explains why infants and those unable to intellectually choose are nonetheless implicated in the fall's consequences—they are part of Adam's lineage. Corporate solidarity in Adam not only locates the root cause of sin but also highlights the corporate dimension of redemption: just as all sinned in Adam, so all may be made alive in Christ (Rom 5:18–19). This corporate structure underscores the scope of salvation: it is a cosmic rescue operation affecting entire communities and cultures, not merely individualized therapy.

2.7.3 Personal responsibility for individual sin

While corporate solidarity explains inherited corruption, Scripture also insists on individual accountability. Ezekiel

34

emphasizes that "the soul who sins shall die" and that each person will bear the consequences of their own transgressions (Ezek 18:20). This principle preserves both God's justice and human dignity: individuals are not merely pawns of a corrupt nature but moral agents responsible for their choices. Metrics of responsibility appear throughout the Gospels, where Jesus commends or rebukes hearers according to their personal responses to His words. The interaction of corporate and individual dimensions in sin and salvation reveals the complexity of God's moral governance: He judges communities and nations, yet each person stands before Him in singular accountability. Comprehensive salvation must therefore address both inherited corruption and personal guilt.

2.7.4 Global implications—every tribe, tongue, and culture

The universality of sin extends beyond personal and corporate dimensions to embrace the globe. God's redemptive purpose encompasses "every tribe and tongue and people and nation" (Rev 5:9), affirming that the need for salvation is not limited to any particular era or geography. From the most remote hunter-gatherer society to the most technologically advanced civilization, no culture has achieved moral perfection or escaped the fall's effects. Ethnographic studies, archaeological discoveries, and cross-cultural surveys all confirm patterns of violence, idolatry, and injustice that testify to our shared human predicament. The Great Commission therefore carries an urgent global mandate: to proclaim salvation to the ends of the earth (Matt 28:19). Only universal proclamation can meet the universal need.

With the universality of the human predicament established, we now ask why salvation must be God-initiated. Section 2.8 will demonstrate the futility of human efforts alone and highlight divine previews that anticipate God's gracious intervention.

2.8 Why Salvation Must Be God-Initiated

2.8.1 The failure of human merit—law exposes rather than cures

Before grace can remedy sin, the law exposes its depth and density, revealing human merit as an inadequate basis for salvation. The apostle Paul explains that the law was given "that every mouth may be stopped and all the world may become accountable to God" (Rom 3:19). Far from empowering people to earn righteousness, the law magnifies sin, showing how every command can be broken in thought, word, or deed. Legalism breeds pride in superficial obedience or despair at inevitable failure. Moreover, historical examples—such as the Pharisees' rigorous rule-keeping—demonstrate how religious systems can harden hearts and obscure the need for divine mercy. The paradox of law, then, is that it exposes guilt without offering the remedy; it is a tutor leading to Christ, not the final answer (Gal 3:24). Human merit collapses under scrutiny, leaving only the need for God's mercy.

2.8.2 Historic previews of divine rescue—Noah, Exodus, Judges

Throughout redemptive history, God provided previews of His saving work, acting unilaterally to rescue sinners. In the flood narrative, Noah and his family were saved not by building the ark themselves but by God's spoken command and sovereign preservation (Gen 6–9). During the Exodus, Pharaoh's armies were powerless against God's deliverance; Israel crossed the sea on dry ground by divine fiat (Exod 14). The era of the Judges further showcased rescue by God's strength rather than human merit, as mighty deliverers like Deborah and Gideon succeeded only by divine empowerment (Judg 4–7). These historical models highlight that salvation has always been an act of God's initiative, preceding human cooperation. When God moves first, humanity's gratitude and faithfulness follow, rather than the other way around.

2.8.3 Prophetic promises of a new covenant

The prophets declared that the ultimate rescue would be more than a repetition of past deliverances; it would involve a new covenant written on human hearts. Jeremiah envisioned a day when God would "put My law within them, and I will write it on their hearts" (Jer 31:33), promising internal transformation rather than external regulations. Ezekiel foretold a re-creation of the human spirit, "I will give you a new heart, and a new spirit I will put within you" (Ezek 36:26). These prophetic assurances pointed to a salvation that addresses sin's root in the heart, not merely its outward symptoms. The necessity of a new covenant underscores that human will must be renewed by divine action, for only God can effect the inward change required for true obedience.

2.8.4 Foreshadowing the necessity of a sin-bearing substitute

Isaiah's portrait of the Suffering Servant vividly anticipates that divine rescue would require vicarious suffering: "He was pierced for our transgressions; He was crushed for our iniquities; upon Him was the chastisement that brought us peace" (Isa 53:5). This foreshadowing makes clear that humanity could never attain salvation through its own efforts; only a substitute bearing the penalty of sin could satisfy divine justice and accomplish redemption. The sacrificial system of Israel—where animals bore the symbolic weight of human sin—pointed forward to this ultimate substitute (Lev 16). Without a sin-bearing victim, the demands of God's justice would remain unmet. Isaiah's prophecy thus underscores the necessity of an atonement that is both fully divine and fully human, ensuring that salvation is both perfect in efficacy and accessible to every sinner.

Having established why humanity desperately needs salvation and why only God can initiate it, the next chapter will explore the unfolding of God's redemptive plan from covenant promise to Christ's atoning work. Chapter 3 will trace the origins of divine grace and prepare the way for the momentous event in which sinners are reconciled to a holy God.

Conclusion

Having surveyed the magnitude of humanity's fall—our bondage to sin, our powerlessness before death, and the universal scope of our guilt—it becomes undeniable that salvation is not an optional add-on but the very air we must breathe. God's holiness and justice stand as unmovable pillars, affirming that sin cannot go unchecked and that every transgression demands either retribution or substitution. The revelation that no human tradition, moral philosophy, or religious ritual can bridge the chasm we ourselves have dug underscores our desperate need for a divine solution. Yet even as the picture of our ruin seems bleakest, Scripture hints at a coming remedy shaped by divine love and mercy. The path forward does not lie in humanity's striving but in God's initiative—a plan woven into covenant promises, rehearsed in history's deliverances, and ultimately fulfilled in the person and work of Christ. As we close this chapter of indictment, we stand ready to turn the page toward the unfolding of that redemptive plan, eager to discover how grace addresses every dimension of our ruin and ushers us into the very life of God.

Chapter 3. Grace Initiated: God's Redemptive Plan

Long before the world existed, the triune God delighted in a plan of rescue born of love rather than human merit. This divine initiative unfolds not as a reaction to our failures but as the eternal purpose of Father, Son, and Spirit to restore what sin marred. Throughout redemptive history, God's grace first whispers through covenants and sacrificial symbols, then roars in the incarnation of the Word, whose life and death accomplish what no law or human effort could. In a wonder that transcends calculation, the cross both satisfies divine justice and unveils boundless mercy, while the empty tomb vindicates the Savior and guarantees that death will not have the final word. From the Day of Pentecost onward, the same Spirit who inaugurated creation now regenerates hearts, convicts of sin, and calls a scattered humanity into one reconciled family. This chapter traces the contours of grace as it moves from heaven's council to earth's mission field, demonstrating that every act of divine rescue is rooted in God's unchanging character and culminates in the promise of ultimate restoration (Eph 2:8–9; Titus 2:11–13).

3.1 Eternal Counsel of the Trinity

3.1.1 Overflow of intra-Trinitarian love

Long before any corner of creation existed, the Father, Son, and Spirit delighted in perfect fellowship, a communion of love so deep that it needed no external object to overflow its joy. The apostles teach that redemption is not a reluctant concession to human failure but the inevitable out-working of God's eternal generosity (John 17:24). In the Father's heart, the Son was treasured and adored, and by the Spirit their mutual delight found expression in creativity and purpose. This intra-Trinitarian love served as the wellspring from which every act of grace would later flow, ensuring that redemption was motivated by delight rather than duty. Theologians call this dynamic *perichoresis*, the mutual indwelling of the divine persons, emphasizing that divine actions emerge from communal generosity rather than solo initiative. Because the Son eternally pleased the Father (Prov 8:30–31), the incarnation did not surprise the Godhead but realized a joy already shared. Every sacrificial act of Christ—His willing descent into human flesh and His self-emptying on the cross—echoes that original delight in the Triune dance. The Spirit, who "searches everything" including the depths of God (1 Cor 2:10), applies this grace in perfect harmony with the Father's will and the Son's work. Thus, the gospel is first of all a love story within the Godhead, a prelude to the grand narrative of cosmic restoration. No human need could have compelled this act; it was born in the overflow of intra-Trinitarian joy, guaranteeing that redemption is grounded in God's unchangeable character.

3.1.2 Election "in Christ before the foundation of the world"

The mystery of election emerges not from fickle human choice but from God's sovereign purpose "in Christ before the foundation of the world" (Eph 1:4–6). This phrase signals that the plan of salvation was neither reactive nor improvised but forged in the timeless will of the Father, who set His love upon a people to be conformed to the image of His Son. Election, then, precedes every human act of faith—it is the theological soil in which repentance and belief take root. Far from undermining responsibility, this doctrine magnifies grace: sinners do not choose God because He is found attractive in themselves, but He is made attractive in Christ's person and work. The security of the believer rests not in fickle feelings but in an immutable decree, guaranteeing that every chosen soul will be brought safely home. Throughout Scripture, election appears alongside covenant promises, demonstrating the consistency of God's purpose from Abraham's calling (Gen 12:1–3) to the final consummation in Revelation. It also safeguards the gospel against merit-based distortion: faith itself is a gift (Phil 1:29), wrought by the same hand that ordained our adoption. The assurance born of election spurs perseverance, for believers rest in a calling that cannot be broken (John 10:28–29). Election's mystery remains veiled to human reasoning, yet its practical effect is evangelical zeal—knowing that God's purposes will not be thwarted fuels missionary courage. By anchoring salvation in Christ before time began, election ensures that divine grace is at once initiated and guaranteed by the Trinity's eternal counsel.

3.1.3 The "Covenant of Redemption" between Father, Son, and Spirit

Embedded within the doctrine of election lies the *Covenant of Redemption*, an intra-Trinitarian agreement whereby the Father appointed the Son to accomplish the work of salvation and the Spirit to apply its benefits. This covenant, though not explicit in a single biblical passage, emerges from the interplay of texts such as Hebrews 10:5–10, where Christ declares His willingness to bear the will of the Father. In this agreement, the Son consents to incarnate, suffer, and die, while the Spirit pledges to empower and preserve the elect. The covenant's triune logic prevents any suggestion that God's love is divided; instead, it demonstrates a flawless cooperation in which each person of the Godhead contributes uniquely to the rescue mission. The Father furnishes the gift, the Son pays the price, and the Spirit administers the blessing—each action flowing from the same divine intent. This framework also illuminates passages that speak of Christ's intercession (Heb 7:25) and the Spirit's sealing ministry (Eph 1:13–14), showing that every stage of salvation was pre-arranged in covenant fellowship. The Covenant of Redemption thus functions as cosmic backstage planning, guaranteeing that the enterprise of grace will succeed. Recognizing this covenant enriches our understanding of God's unity and the seamless progression from decreed purpose to enacted salvation.

Having observed how grace originates in the eternal fellowship and purpose of the Trinity, we next trace how that divine counsel unfolds across redemptive history through successive covenants, each building toward the arrival of the Messiah.

3.2 Covenantal Storyline of Scripture

3.2.1 Edenic promise—proto-evangelium

Immediately after the fall, God uttered a promise that would echo through every subsequent act of mercy: the proto-evangelium in Genesis 3:15. This first hint of redemption revealed that the Seed of the woman would one day crush the serpent's head, countering the serpent's bruising of His heel. In doing so, God introduced a Messianic hope anchored in cosmic conflict, where evil's power would be decisively broken. This promise shaped Adam and Eve's exile, transforming a sentence of judgment into the first glimmer of grace. Throughout the patriarchal narratives, Jewish interpreters recognized this motif, anticipating a redeemer who would fulfill the promise embedded in Eden's soil. The proto-evangelium's significance lies in its immediate birth from divine justice tempered by mercy—a pattern that recurs in each covenantal stage. By embedding redemption at the point of highest despair, God signaled that His plan would not merely restore Eden but transcend it. The first gospel announcement thus serves as the keystone for all later covenants, anchoring the storyline in a divine commitment to rescue.

3.2.2 Noahic stability of creation for redemptive history

Following the flood, God renewed His commitment to fallen humanity and a corrupted world through the Noahic covenant, promising never again to destroy the earth by flood (Gen 9:11–17). The sign of the rainbow testified to divine faithfulness and introduced stability into the unfolding drama of redemption. In preserving creation, God affirmed that His plan of grace would proceed across generations, unmoved by ephemeral wickedness. This covenant extended mercy to all living beings, countering the permanent destruction their sin would otherwise merit. It also reinforced the pattern of covenant and sign—a pattern that would later manifest in circumcision, Passover, and baptism. By safeguarding the earth, God laid the stage for the calling of Abraham and the emergence of a people through whom blessing would flow. The Noahic covenant thus illustrates that grace persists even amid pervasive corruption, ensuring that redemption's storyline remains intact.

3.2.3 Abrahamic pledge of global blessing

When God called Abram out of Ur, He inaugurated the Abrahamic covenant: "In you all the families of the earth shall be blessed" (Gen 12:3; Gal 3:8). This promise expanded grace beyond individual pardon, envisioning a people through whom divine blessing would radiate worldwide. Abraham's faith was reckoned as righteousness (Gen 15:6), modeling how election and promise converge in trust rather than merit. The sign of this covenant—circumcision—marked a people set apart for mission, a holy seed in the midst of pagan nations. Over time, Abraham's descendants wrestled with obedience yet never outgrew the original pledge of blessing to the nations. The Abrahamic covenant thus shifts the narrative from promise to people, demonstrating that God's redemptive plan always involves a community destined to bear witness to His grace.

3.2.4 Mosaic covenant—law as tutor to Christ

At Sinai, God bound Himself to Israel through a covenant anchored in the giving of the law (Exod 19–24; Gal 3:19–25). This covenant introduced moral and ceremonial ordinances that functioned both as a guide to holy living and as a tutor pointing to Christ. While the law codified God's character for His people, it also revealed humanity's inability to fulfill divine standards, thereby intensifying the longing for a greater Deliverer. Sacrifices and festivals performed under Sinai foreshadowed the ultimate once-for-all sacrifice the Messiah would offer. Thus, the Mosaic covenant occupies a dual role: it commands obedience and simultaneously prepares hearts for a superior covenant of grace.

3.2.5 Davidic throne anticipating Messianic rule

God's promise to David of an everlasting throne (2 Sam 7:12–16) shifted redemptive focus toward regal fulfillment in the Son of David. While Israel's kings often failed, the Davidic covenant assured a future ruler whose reign would combine justice and peace. Prophets like Isaiah and Micah drew upon this promise to extol a coming King whose dominion would encompass nations and establish universal righteousness. The sign of this covenant was royal lineage—David's descendants—yet its ultimate realization lay in the Messiah's kingly office. By including the Davidic promise in the covenantal sequence, Scripture weaves together grace and governance, anticipating a kingdom that unites sovereignty and salvation.

3.2.6 New covenant promise of internal renewal

Jeremiah's prophecy of a new covenant etched on human hearts (Jer 31:31–34) marked the summit of covenantal progression. Unlike earlier covenants that relied on external statutes, this promise envisioned an inward transformation by which God Himself would write His law within His people. Ezekiel's parallel vision of a new spirit and a new heart (Ezek 36:26–27) underscored the necessity of regeneration for true obedience. The new covenant thus synthesizes every previous promise—bringing forgiveness (Jer 31:34), enabling faith (Heb 8:10), and inaugurating the age of the Spirit. It serves as the hinge between Old Testament anticipation and New Testament fulfillment, guaranteeing that God's redemptive plan culminates in an unbreakable union between divine grace and human experience.

With the covenantal promises mapped from Eden through Jeremiah, we now examine how Israel's worship and national history repeatedly foreshadowed the coming Messiah, preparing the stage for the incarnation.

3.3 Foreshadows in Israel's Worship and History

3.3.1 Passover lamb and the logic of substitution

Every spring, Israel gathered at twilight to participate in the Passover, a festival commemorating divine rescue from Egyptian bondage (Exod 12; 1 Cor 5:7). Each household selected an unblemished lamb, the slain blood on doorposts declaring that judgment would pass over obedient families. This ritual underscored the principle of substitution: an innocent victim bearing the penalty of the guilty. The lamb's flesh nourished the people physically, yet its blood spoke of spiritual preservation. Generations of Israelites saw in this act not only a memorial of past freedom but also a prophecy of the Lamb of God who would once and for all deliver from sin's dominion. The Passover thus became a living symbol of grace, instilling in God's people a visceral understanding of sacrificial rescue.

3.3.2 Sacrificial system and priestly mediation

The Levitical system institutionalized daily and annual sacrifices for sin, where priests served as mediators between a holy God and a guilty people (Lev 4; Heb 9:11–14). Each offering—burnt, sin, or guilt—provided a picture of Christ's multifaceted atonement: consecration, propitiation, and restitution. The high priest's entry into the Holy of Holies once a year symbolized the once-in-a-lifetime reconciliation necessary for communion with God. Through repeated rituals, Israel was reminded of both the seriousness of sin and the necessity of a perfect Priest to secure eternal pardon. These ceremonies taught that human hands could not effect genuine forgiveness; only the blood of an unblemished Mediator could satisfy divine demands. The sacrificial system thus foreshadowed the climactic priesthood of Jesus, unveiling the logic of substitutionary atonement and intercession.

3.3.3 Exodus pattern of deliverance

Israel's exodus from Egypt provided a living drama of salvation that shaped national identity and theological imagination (Exod 14; 1 Cor 10:1–4). God's miraculous interventions—plagues, parting sea, provision in the wilderness—demonstrated His power to liberate slaves and lead them into covenant relationship. This pattern of rescue and guidance recurred in Joshua's conquest, the judges' deliverances, and the restoration under Ezra and Nehemiah. Each historic salvation narrated God's covenant faithfulness and rehearsed motifs of bondage, deliverance, and inheritance. The exodus thus served as a concrete template for anticipating a greater liberation from sin and death. Believers in Christ would later recognize His cross and resurrection as the definitive exodus, where the new Israel crosses from slavery to freedom under a better Moses (Heb 3:1–6).

3.3.4 Prophetic portraits of Servant and King

Beyond rituals and histories, the prophets painted vivid portraits of God's coming Servant and King, unveiling the character and mission of the Messiah. Isaiah described a Servant who would bear our infirmities and bear the judgment due sinners (Isa 42; 53). Zechariah envisioned a humble King riding on a donkey, inaugurating an era of peace (Zech 9:9). These messages pierced the complacency of Israel, exposing religious formalism and pointing to an unexpected Deliverer. The prophetic corpus survey reveals that Israel's worship life was always eyed toward fulfillment in one who would embody servant-sacrifice and sovereign rule. Thus, Israel's worship and history functioned as preparatory classrooms, readying the people for the arrival of the incarnate Word.

Having traced grace's anticipation in Israel's worship and prophetic voice, we turn now to the climactic event: the incarnation of the eternal Word, where God's redemptive plan takes human form.

3.4 Incarnation: The Word Made Flesh

3.4.1 Virgin birth and true humanity

In the fulness of time, the Second Person of the Trinity assumed human nature through a virgin birth, uniting deity and humanity in one person (Luke 1:35; Phil 2:6–8). This miracle validated that salvation required a mediator fully divine—able to bear infinite wrath—and fully human—able to represent our race. By entering our world without defect or corruption, the incarnate Word sanctified human flesh, preparing it to be the instrument of divine action. His human birth also fulfilled Old Testament prophecies that Messiah would come from the lineage of David yet born of a virgin (Isa 7:14; Rom 1:3–4). In His early years, Christ's perfect development in wisdom and stature revealed how redeemed humanity ought to grow in grace. The virgin birth thus safeguards the uniqueness and sinlessness of Christ's person, ensuring that His life and death qualify Him as the perfect substitute for sinners.

3.4.2 Active obedience fulfilling the law

Throughout His earthly ministry, Jesus lived in flawless conformity to the law's every demand, fulfilling both its letter and its spirit (Matt 5:17). His active obedience—unbroken by any hint of selfish motive—accumulated merit that would be imputed to believers. In contrast to Israel's historical failures under Sinai, Jesus succeeded in perfect righteousness as the last and greatest Israelite. His sinless life also provided an example for disciples to imitate, teaching that righteousness is not human achievement but the fruit of union with Him. At every turn, He demonstrated mercy without compromising justice, upholding the law's intent while revealing its fullest meaning. By His active obedience, Christ rendered the law's condemnation moot for those united to Him, transferring to believers the perfection He alone possessed.

3.4.3 Representative headship—Second Adam

Scripture presents Christ as the Second Adam, whose obedience undoes the first Adam's disobedience (Rom 5:17–19). Whereas humanity's headship under Adam brought sin and death to all his offspring, Christ's headship ushers in life and righteousness to everyone united with Him. This representative headship means that believers participate in His victory through faith, being counted as crucified, buried, and resurrected with Him (Rom 6:3–5). The image of the Second Adam also deepens our understanding of corporate solidarity: as Adam's sin made death universal, so Christ's righteousness extends life universally to His elect. This parallelism underscores that salvation is not merely a private transaction but a cosmic recapitulation, resetting creation through the obedience of one. Christ's role as Representative Head thus guarantees that His work has definitive power to reverse the curse and inaugurate new creation.

Having explored how grace found flesh in the person of Jesus—through miraculous birth, perfect obedience, and federal headship—we are now prepared to examine the culmination of His mission in the atoning work of the cross.

3.5 The Cross: Obedience unto Death

3.5.1 Substitutionary atonement and propitiation

On the cross, Christ stood in the sinner's place, bearing the penalty we deserved and satisfying the righteous demands of a holy God (Isa 53:5–6). His body was wounded, not for any personal failing, but so that our wounds might be healed, demonstrating that divine love and justice meet in sacrificial exchange. This substitution was not cosmetic or symbolic alone; it was real and effectual, accomplishing full atonement that needs no repetition. Propitiation means that Christ's death turns away God's wrath, not by bribery or coercion, but by fulfilling the just requirement that sin be paid for. The New Testament repeatedly affirms that Jesus "died for our sins," indicating that our guilt was imputed to Him and His righteousness imputed to us (2 Cor 5:21). In His substitutive suffering, He endured the full weight of divine judgment, absorbing the fury that our transgressions merited. Yet He did so voluntarily: He was not an involuntary victim but the willing Lamb "led to the slaughter" (Isa 53:7). This willingness underscores the depth of the Father's delight in the Son's obedience, echoing the intra-Trinitarian covenant. As sinners receive Christ by faith, they are united to His death, so that their own liability is abolished in Him. Thus, substitutionary atonement lies at the heart of the gospel, revealing that salvation is purchased, not by human merit, but by Christ's meritorious work.

3.5.2 Triumph over powers—Christus Victor motif

Beyond paying a legal price, the cross enacted a cosmic victory, disarming principalities and powers through Christ's shameful death (Col 2:14–15). In that moment of apparent defeat, the Lamb overthrew the strongman's grip, nullifying the spiritual forces that held humankind captive. Far from being a defeat, the cross was the decisive blow in the war against evil, where the champion allowed Himself to be bound in order to bind the enemy. Early church writers dubbed this the Christus Victor motif, emphasizing that Christ's death and resurrection were a campaign of liberation. The shattered gates of Hades and the trampled serpent's head testify to this triumph, assuring believers that no spiritual foe can ultimately prevail against the risen Lord. Scripture invites us to view every cross-bearing Christian life as participating in this victory, sharing in Christ's conquest over sin, death, and darkness. Because He disarmed the powers, believers now stand in authority over demonic influences—not by their own strength but by virtue of union with the Victorious One. The cross thus serves as the strategic center of redemptive history, where grace meets conflict and emerges in glory.

3.5.3 Covenant ratified in blood

When Jesus instituted the Lord's Supper, He declared that His blood was "the blood of the covenant, poured out for many for the forgiveness of sins" (Matt 26:28). This language echoes God's earlier covenants, where blood sealed solemn agreements, signaling irrevocable commitment. In the heavenly sanctuary model of Hebrews, Christ's blood enters the true Holy of Holies, ratifying a superior covenant that grants direct access to God (Heb 9:15–22). The sacrificial system under Sinai foreshadowed this climactic moment, where the high priest's once-a-year offering looked forward to a better blood that would cleanse the conscience permanently. Christ's shed blood thus inaugurates a covenant written not on tablets of stone but on human hearts, fulfilling Jeremiah's prophecy of internal renewal. This ratification means that every believer is bound to Christ in an unbreakable alliance, secured by the price He paid. No force can dissolve a covenant ratified in the life-giving blood of the Son, ensuring that those whom He redeems remain His possession. As worshipers partake of communion, they reenact their inclusion in this covenant, proclaiming the Lord's death until He comes.

Having surveyed the cross as both substitution and triumph, and seen the new covenant sealed in blood, we turn next to the resurrection and ascension—events that vindicate Christ's work and establish His ongoing reign.

3.6 Resurrection and Ascension

3.6.1 Vindication of the Son and validation of the cross

The resurrection vindicates Christ as the righteous Judge and confirms that His death achieved its intended purpose (Acts 2:24–36). When the Father raised the Son, He declared His acceptance of the atoning sacrifice and demonstrated that death had no claim on One who had never sinned. This vindication silences every charge from accuser or skeptic, for God's decisive act endorses Christ's worthiness as Savior. It also retroactively validates every propitiatory act on the cross:

what looked like defeat was in fact the prelude to resurrection triumph. Believers therefore anchor their faith not in myth or moral teaching alone, but in the historic event of a risen Lord, whose empty tomb proclaims divine power unleashed. The resurrection also inaugurates new-creation life, promising that those united to Christ will share in His victory over the grave. In vindicating the Son, God beckons sinners to trust in a Savior who has proven His authority over sin and death.

3.6.2 Firstfruits of a new creation

Paul calls Christ the "firstfruits" of those who have fallen asleep, framing His resurrection as the beginning of a larger harvest of redeemed humanity (1 Cor 15:20–23). In agricultural imagery, the firstfruits are a guarantee of the full crop to come, and so Christ's rising is a foretaste of the general resurrection at His return. This typology connects Christ's bodily renewal with the future transformation of creation itself, suggesting that redemption extends beyond souls to the entire cosmos. The firstfruits motif also comforts believers in mourning, affirming that death is not the final word but a temporary sleep before gathering into glory. As the firstfruits ascend in our foretaste, so the rest will follow in due season, sharing in the incorruptible life of the risen Lord. Thus, the resurrection letters ecology: it reassures the church that redemption has begun and will one day be consummated in the full restoration of all things.

3.6.3 Heavenly session and royal intercession

After His resurrection, Christ ascended to the Father's right hand, where He corresponds to Israel's enthroned King and High Priest simultaneously (Heb 7:25; Eph 1:20–22). This session is not idle sovereignty but an active reign characterized by intercession for His people, ensuring that every provision of the cross is applied. From this royal vantage, Christ mediates grace, presenting His blood before the Father on behalf of believers. His intercession bridges the gap between heaven and earth, supplying strength for weakness and advocacy for doubt. As exalted Lord, He also dispatches the Spirit, empowering the church for service until all enemies are under His feet. The session underscores that Christ's redemptive work continues; the cross and empty tomb are complemented by ongoing priestly care. This dynamic royal-priestly ministry ensures that grace flows perpetually from the throne, sustaining the pilgrim people of God.

With Christ's exalted reign securing the benefits of cross and resurrection, we now consider the Spirit's ministry at Pentecost—His convicting and drawing work that applies salvation to sinner's hearts.

3.7 Pentecost and the Spirit's Pre-conversion Ministry

3.7.1 Outpoured Spirit inaugurates the age of mission

On the day of Pentecost, the promised Spirit descended in rushing wind and tongues of fire, inaugurating the church's global mission (Acts 2:16–21). This dramatic outpouring fulfilled Joel's prophecy of a Spirit poured on all flesh, signaling that the new covenant era had dawned. The Spirit's arrival transcended national and linguistic barriers, as diverse pilgrims heard the gospel in their own languages. This universal gifting underscored that salvation was no longer confined to ethnic Israel but offered to every nation. The Spirit's presence empowered the apostles to preach with boldness, perform signs, and establish communities marked by love and unity. Pentecost thus marks the transition from covenant promise to worldwide proclamation, reminding the church that grace compels outreach. The missionary impulse of the Spirit continues today, driving God's people to evangelize until the ends of the earth.

3.7.2 Conviction of sin, righteousness, judgment

Before the Spirit regenerates, He first convicts the world of sin, righteousness, and judgment, preparing hearts to receive the gospel (John 16:8–11). This conviction penetrates the depths of human resistance, exposing hypocrisy and stirring awareness of guilt. It reveals what sin truly is—rebellion against a holy God—and shows the insufficiency of self-justification. By spotlighting righteousness, the Spirit points to Christ as the only source of genuine right standing before God. Conviction of judgment reminds sinners that they face a real penalty, intensifying the urgency of repentance. Far from coercing belief, this work respects human agency while dismantling every excuse. The Spirit's convicting ministry thus lays the groundwork for conversion, ensuring that faith arises in an informed and humble heart.

3.7.3 Drawing and regenerating the elect

In God's redemptive plan, the Spirit not only convicts but also draws and regenerates the elect, initiating the new birth (John 6:44; Titus 3:5). Drawing involves the Spirit's irresistibly attracting grace, granting sensitivity to God's voice and messages. Regeneration is a sovereign act in which the Spirit imparts new life, transforming dead hearts into living temples of God. This spiritual rebirth is not gradual improvement but an instantaneous impartation of divine life, enabling faith and repentance. Regeneration also reconfigures the affections, so that love for God becomes the believer's dominant motive. As the Spirit renovates the inner person, He plants the seeds of sanctification that will grow throughout the believer's life. This pre-conversion ministry assures us that salvation is from start to finish a work of grace, initiated and sustained by the Spirit's power.

Having explored how the Spirit convicts, draws, and regenerates, we now turn to how grace spills outward in the church's ongoing mission to all peoples.

3.8 The Universal Call and Ongoing Mission

3.8.1 Gospel to Jew first and also to Gentile

Paul declares the gospel "to the Jew first and also to the Greek," affirming the priority of Israel in redemptive history while extending invitation to Gentiles alike (Rom 1:16). This order honors God's covenantal promises to Abraham and

David, recognizing that the Messiah would emerge from Jewish soil. Yet the inclusion of Greeks illustrates that the gospel transcends ethnic boundaries, breaking down dividing walls of hostility. The church's posture therefore combines faithful witness in local contexts with intentional outreach to those beyond the cultural perimeter. This universal call compels believers to navigate cultural differences, contextualizing the message without altering its truth. As Jews and Gentiles worship together, they demonstrate that grace unites former enemies into one family. The universal scope of the call ensures that every tribe and tongue has opportunity to respond, fulfilling the Abrahamic vision of global blessing.

3.8.2 Apostolic commission and global disciple-making

Before ascending, Jesus entrusted the apostles with a commission: "Go therefore and make disciples of all nations" (Matt 28:18–20). This charge encompasses proclamation of the Word, baptism, and teaching obedience—an integrated process of evangelism and formation. The apostles modeled this pattern through missionary journeys, church planting, and mentorship of emerging leaders. They established communities where new believers were nurtured in doctrine, ethics, and fellowship. This holistic approach to disciple-making continues to inform evangelistic strategy: conversion without subsequent instruction leaves faith shallow and vulnerable. The Great Commission thus affirms that grace calls for both immediate response and lifelong growth, carried out in a community that embodies the kingdom's values.

3.8.3 People of God as embassy of reconciliation

Paul describes the church as ambassadors of Christ, entrusted with the ministry of reconciliation (2 Cor 5:18–20). As representatives of a different kingdom, believers bear God's presence into every sphere of society, proclaiming peace with God and laying down lives in service to others. This ambassadorial role involves both word and deed: preaching the gospel alongside acts of compassion, justice, and mercy. In so doing, the church displays the reconciling power of grace, attracting observers to the transformative gospel.

Embassies operate under the authority of their sending nation; likewise, the church's authority derives from Christ's lordship. This dual identity—as sojourners and ambassadors—frames Christian engagement in the world until Christ returns.

3.8.4 Suffering and perseverance as missional witness

Following apostolic example, the church has often advanced most effectively under persecution, as suffering refines faith and emboldens witness (Phil 1:29–30). Martyrdom and hardship have served as powerful sermons, demonstrating that grace sustains even in the face of hostility and death. Suffering cultivates solidarity with the oppressed and credibility before skeptical observers who see a faith that does not crumble. Perseverance under trial provides a living testimony to the gospel's sufficiency, confirming Christ's promise that "in the world you will have tribulation, but take heart, I have overcome the world" (John 16:33). The missionary movement, past and present, flourishes when the church embraces hardship as part of its calling, trusting that grace empowers endurance and refines character. Thus, suffering and perseverance become indispensable elements of global mission, showcasing grace under fire.

Having traced grace from Pentecost to global witness, we now consider how God guarantees the believer's perseverance and the ultimate consummation of His redemptive plan.

3.9 Grace Guaranteed: Perseverance and Consummation

3.9.1 Spirit-sealed security for believers

From the moment of conversion, believers are sealed with the Holy Spirit as a down payment of their inheritance (Eph 1:13–14). This seal signifies God's ownership and protects the redeemed from the finality of rejection. In ancient Near Eastern practice, a seal on a contract or letter guaranteed its authenticity and inviolability; similarly, the Spirit's seal authenticates every believer before the throne. He illuminates the assurance of salvation, testifying with our spirits that we are God's children (Rom 8:16). This internal witness provides confidence amid doubts, anchoring hope not in fluctuating emotions but in the Spirit's abiding presence. The seal also anticipates the full redemption of body and soul at Christ's return, assuring believers that nothing can nullify God's promise.

3.9.2 Christ's priestly intercession ensures completion

Christ's priestly ministry continues unabated in heaven, where He intercedes for His people (John 17:11; Heb 10:14). His advocacy is not perfunctory but fervent, rooted in the same obedience that led Him to the cross. As High Priest, He presents the merits of His atoning work to the Father, securing daily grace for weakness and strength for temptation. This ongoing intercession ensures that every temptation faced by believers has already been addressed by the victorious Savior. Even when faith falters, Christ's prayers uphold the elect, guaranteeing that none can pluck them from His hand. His intercession thus undergirds perseverance, making certain that the salvation He initiated will reach completion.

3.9.3 New-creation horizon—everything summed up in Christ

The grand finale of redemptive history looms on the horizon: the new heavens and new earth where God dwells with His people (Rev 21:5; Eph 1:10). In this consummation, every strand of grace—election, covenant, incarnation, cross, Spirit, mission—converges in perfect harmony. Sin, mourning, and death will be eradicated, and redemption's design will be fully realized. Believers will inhabit resurrected bodies, engage in unending worship, and exercise restored stewardship over creation. This eschatological hope empowers present obedience, for it transforms trials into labors of love and service. With the consummation assured, grace becomes the lens through which every moment of history is interpreted, giving meaning to suffering, zeal to mission, and confidence in ultimate victory.

Conclusion

As we close this survey of God's redemptive initiative, we stand in awe of a grace that originates in the depths of divine fellowship and reaches to the depths of human need. The narrative of covenant promises, incarnation, atoning sacrifice, victorious resurrection, and Spirit-empowered mission reveals a seamless tapestry woven by God's hand. Grace does not merely forgive but transforms, equipping the church to bear witness until the age ends. What has been begun by Christ and the Spirit will not be abandoned; every rescued soul, every renewed community, and every foretaste of the coming kingdom point toward a consummation in which God's purposes are fully realized. With this panoramic vision of grace before us, we now turn to the heart of personal salvation—the moment when an individual sinner is declared righteous—anticipating the profound blessings of justification by faith alone (Rom 5:8; Gal 4:4–5).

Chapter 4. Saved Once: The Doctrine of Justification

Justification stands at the heart of the Christian gospel, declaring that guilty sinners are declared righteous before a holy God not by their own merit but solely through Christ's finished work. In this divine courtroom drama, the believer receives a verdict that permanently cancels condemnation and inaugurates new standing before the Judge of all the earth. Far from a gradual process, justification is a once-for-all declaration that anchors assurance and shapes every aspect of the Christian life. When faith grasps this gift, it discovers unshakable peace, no longer condemned under the law's condemnation, yet restored to its intended relationship with the Creator. This chapter explores how divine righteousness is credited, how faith functions as the means of reception, and how the believer's union with Christ secures a legal standing that transcends human frailty. Understanding justification is essential not only for personal assurance but also for a vibrant, gratitude-driven witness in the world.

4.1 The Courtroom of God — Definition & Legal Background

Forensic versus transformative categories clarified

Justification is fundamentally a forensic act, a legal declaration by God that pronounces guilty sinners righteous through the merit of Christ rather than any inherent change within them. In divine court imagery, the Judge of all the earth enters into the sinner's case and issues a verdict based entirely on the work of another. This contrasts with transformative categories such as sanctification, which describe the gradual renewing of the believer's nature. Yet the courtroom act and the transformative process remain distinct: one is instantaneous and complete, while the other is progressive and lifelong. By understanding justification as forensic, Christians grasp that their acceptance before God does not hinge on subjective feelings or fluctuating spiritual performance. Rather, it rests on the objective reality that Christ's perfect obedience and sacrifice satisfy divine justice once for all (Rom 3:24–26). This legal framework also clarifies why good works cannot earn standing before God; they lack the requisite merit to appease divine wrath. Furthermore, distinguishing forensic justification from relational fellowship highlights that believers, though positionally declared righteous, still pursue experiential communion with God. The courtroom verdict secures their status; the ongoing transformation deepens their stature. Recognizing this distinction guards against conflating salvation's gift with the necessary fruit that flows from it. By framing justification in forensic terms, Scripture comforts wavering consciences with the certainty of acquittal and root out attempts to blend law-keeping with the free grace of faith.

Old-Testament legal scenes as prototypes

In the Old Testament, various legal procedures foreshadow the doctrine of justification, offering vivid prototypes of divine verdicts. When disputes arose between Israelites, Levitical judges heard evidence, weighed testimony, and rendered decisions that brought peace to the community (Deut 25:1).

These human tribunals, though flawed, reflect the heavenly courtroom in miniature, where God Himself adjudicates cases with perfect wisdom. The prophet Isaiah depicts the Lord as a litigant who attends His own trial, ensuring no false accusation can stand (Isa 50:8). Such imagery underlines the reassurance that God governs His court with unfailing integrity. Moreover, the public nature of Old-Testament judgments—pronouncements made at the city gate—anticipates the public declaration of righteousness in justification. The accused faced collection of evidence and a binding verdict; the believer approaches God's throne only in Christ's name and emerges declared justified. Even the sacrificial system bore legal overtones: blood offerings symbolized the removal of guilt, pointing ahead to Christ's ultimate atoning sacrifice. These prototypes teach that justification does not spring from spiritual mysticism but from a divine legal process. By examining these ancient legal scenes, the church discerns the continuity between God's dealings with Israel and His granting of righteousness to justified sinners.

Paul's term dikaioō *in Greco-Roman jurisprudence*

When the apostle Paul employs the Greek term *dikaioō* in his letters, he taps into familiar Greco-Roman legal language to communicate the concept of justification. In secular courts, *dikaioō* signified a judge's declaration of innocence, absolving the accused from charges based on presented evidence. Paul repurposes this term to describe God's act of declaring sinners righteous on account of Christ's obedience, establishing an immediate resonance for Gentile readers accustomed to courtroom parlance (Rom 4:5; Gal 2:16). This linguistic choice underscores the non-religious, civil nature of justification—it is less about spiritual transformation and more about standing before a judge. Yet Paul expands the term's nuance by rooting it in divine action rather than human deliberation, emphasizing that the evidence for acquittal is Christ's life, death, and resurrection. The certitude of *dikaioō* in Paul's usage leaves no room for partial verdicts; justification is either granted in full or not at all. This contrasts with human courts, where verdicts can be appealed or overturned; divine justification is irrevocable. Understanding Paul's appropriation of *dikaioō* clarifies his insistence that justification is by faith and not by works, for no human achievement can warrant the Lord's favorable decree. By tracing the term through its cultural context, readers appreciate the boldness of Paul's claim: that God Himself adopts legal categories and transforms them to assure believers of their righteous standing.

4.2 Double Imputation — Righteousness Credited & Sin Removed

Adam's guilt reckoned to humanity

The doctrine of double imputation begins with the reality that Adam, as federal head of humanity, represented his progeny in the Garden. When he disobeyed, his guilt was legally charged to every descendant, rendering all men and women under the condemnation of sin (Rom 5:12–14). This collective reckoning explains why even infants, incapable of personal transgression, inherit a fallen nature subject to death. The imagery is that of a legal ledger: Adam's offense registers against each person's account. This legal mechanism highlights the seriousness of sin and justifies humanity's need for an equivalent remedy; if guilt can be imputed by a representative act, so can righteousness. The federal principle demonstrates that sin's reach is structural, not merely episodic. This understanding dissolves notions of moral demerit based solely on individual actions and grounds the necessity of a Savior whose representative act will overturn Adam's verdict. It also illuminates the intensity of divine justice, for God treats humanity's race as spiritually one, requiring a solution that addresses the corporate dimension of sin.

Christ's active obedience counted to believers

In parallel to Adam's disobedience, Christ's active obedience—His perfect fulfillment of the law—is credited to believers upon faith. His life of sinless devotion generated a surplus of merit, imputed to those united with Him, so that God views His people as having kept every command (Phil 3:9). This accounting of righteousness treats the believer's file as if Christ's spotless perfection were their own. Thus, double imputation entails not only the removal of Adam's guilt but also the transplanting of Christ's righteousness into their account. This gracious reckoning abolishes the legal barrier that sin erected and grants access to divine privileges previously reserved for the sinless. By crediting Christ's obedience rather than human effort, God upholds His law's integrity while demonstrating mercy. The believer's confidence in justification arises from this guaranteed transfer, secure in a righteousness that no failure can diminish, for it rests wholly on Christ's fulfilled obedience.

"The great exchange" grounded in substitution

The language of substitution undergirds double imputation: Christ stands in our place, bearing our sin so that we might receive His righteousness. Paul's declaration that God made Him "to be sin who knew no sin, so that in Him we might become the righteousness of God" (2 Cor 5:21) frames justification as a two-way transaction. This great exchange involves Christ's volitional assumption of our sin and His willing impartation of His righteousness. It is not a blending of moral qualities but a definitive swap: our unrighteousness for His perfection. The cross enacts this exchange; it is the hinge upon which imputation turns. By emphasizing substitution, Scripture assures that no human merit dilutes the exchange— Christ's perfect person and work alone effect the transfer. This doctrine reinforces the forensic nature of justification, for exchanges occur within legal frameworks, ensuring that both guilt removal and righteousness credit are accomplished with divine authority and precision.

With double imputation established—Adam's guilt removed and Christ's righteousness credited—we now examine how faith functions as the sole instrument through which sinners receive this justifying verdict.

4.3 Faith Alone, Grace Alone — The Instrument of Justification

Nature of saving faith: knowledge, assent, trust

Saving faith comprises at least three inseparable elements: intellectual assent to gospel truth, heartfelt trust in Christ, and a willing commitment to rely on Him alone for salvation. Knowledge involves accurate understanding that Jesus is the promised Messiah who accomplished atonement through His death and resurrection (John 1:12). Assent affirms that these truths are indeed factual and authoritative, rejecting any notion that they are mere opinions. Trust goes deeper: it personalizes Christ's work, prompting the sinner to rest wholly on Him for pardon and acceptance. This trust is not mere emotional enthusiasm but a reasoned confidence supported by the Spirit's witness. Scripture commends faith's primacy in justification while never divorcing it from understanding, ensuring that saving belief arises from genuine knowledge rather than blind leap. The believer's journey begins when faith grasps grace, emerging from the synergy of mind, heart, and will.

Repentance as faith's inseparable twin

Repentance and faith are two sides of the same coin, each authenticating the other. Repentance involves a sincere turning from sin—an admission of guilt and a rejection of self-righteousness—rooted in sorrow for having offended God. It is impossible to claim faith while cherishing the very sins Christ died to atone, for faith reorients affections toward the Savior. Conversely, repentance without faith in Christ's substitutionary work risks devolving into mere moralism, as it attempts to remedy sin by human resolve alone. Acts distinguishes these elements yet consistently links them in the call, "repent and believe," underscoring that true conversion entails both a negative turning from sin and a positive turning to Christ. This inseparability safeguards the purity of justification, ensuring that faith is not a detached intellectual exercise but a life-transforming reliance on divine grace.

Faith as instrument, not meritorious cause

Scripture declares that justification is by grace through faith, not by works, so that no one may boast (Eph 2:8–9). Faith serves as the instrument—a means or channel—through which Christ's righteousness is received. It contributes nothing to God's decision to justify; rather, it appropriates the righteousness already accomplished. A meritorious cause, by contrast, would imply that faith itself earns salvation, yet Scripture rejects any human contribution to earning God's favor. Even the faith enabling conversion is Himself a gift, wrought by the Spirit's regenerating work. This distinction ensures that the believer's confidence rests in divine action and not human performance. Faith's instrumental role highlights its indispensability without attributing to it any intrinsic merit. By affirming the solo work of grace, the doctrine of justification magnifies God's free favor and safeguards against any drift into works-righteousness.

Having explored how saving faith receives the gift of justification, we next consider the believer's union with Christ as the relational reality that secures the justifying verdict.

4.4 Union with Christ & the Justifying Verdict

Mystical and covenantal union defined

Believers are mystically and covenantally united to Christ, forming one new organism in which His life and righteousness become theirs (Eph 1:3–6). This union is mystical in that it transcends empirical explanation, yet it is covenantal because it rests on divine promise and is activated by faith. Through union, Jesus becomes the believer's representative, and all His benefits flow into their experience. Paul describes this bond as akin to marriage: just as two become one flesh, so the believer is ingrafted into the body of Christ. This oneness ensures that Christ's death is counted as the believer's death and His resurrection as their resurrection. The covenantal language underscores that union is not optional but the divinely instituted framework within which justification operates.

Temporal application of an eternal decree

While the decree of justification was determined in eternity past, its application to individuals occurs at the moment of faith, connecting the timeless decision of God to temporal human experience (2 Tim 1:9). This aspect of divine providence highlights that God's eternal counsel finds concrete expression in history. When a sinner believes, the eternal verdict descends into time, altering their legal standing before God. This temporal appropriation does not restart the divine decree but actualizes it for each recipient. In this way, justification bridges eternity and history, ensuring that God's immutable purpose meets human need in real time. Believers thus partake of an eternal reality through a momentary act of faith.

Baptism and the Lord's Table as signs, not causes, of union

Sacraments such as baptism and the Lord's Supper signify the believer's union with Christ and the benefits of justification (Rom 6:3–4; 1 Cor 10:16). Baptism symbolizes the believer's participation in the death and resurrection of Jesus, marking them as justified and clothed in His righteousness. The Lord's Table commemorates the new covenant and proclaims the efficacy of His shed blood for forgiveness. However, these rites do not effect union or justification; they visibly seal what faith has already accomplished. By distinguishing signs from causes, the church upholds the centrality of faith and averts reliance on ritual for salvation. Sacraments thus nourish and confirm union, reinforcing the believer's identity as one with Christ, already justified by grace.

With union securing the justifying verdict and sacraments affirming it, we now turn to how obedience and good works relate to a justified life without undermining the sola fide principle.

4.5 Justification & Works — The Role of Obedience

4.5.1 Harmonizing Paul and James on "faith without works"

Paul's insistence that we are justified by faith apart from works (Rom 3:28) can seem to conflict with James's declaration that "faith without works is dead" (Jas 2:17). Yet a closer look reveals complementary emphases rather than contradiction. Paul addresses the ground of our initial standing before God—how sinners receive a righteous verdict—while James addresses the manifestation of true faith in the life of the believer. Genuine faith, Paul would agree, inevitably produces action; otherwise it remains an intellectual assent devoid of spiritual vitality. James uses the language of works to demonstrate that a claim to faith unaccompanied by life-changing obedience is self-refuting, akin to a heart in hibernation rather than a living spring. Neither apostle diminishes the other's point: Paul never suggests that faith without follow-through is acceptable, and James never implies that works can earn righteousness. Instead, the two combine to show that justification is by faith alone and that that faith is never alone—it is always accompanied by the fruit of obedience. Recognizing the different contexts—justification's courtroom versus sanctification's workshop—reconciles their messages and preserves both the free gift of grace and the necessity of a faith that transforms. This harmony reminds us that while no work can purchase our justification, a faith that truly justifies will express itself in the obedience of love.

4.5.2 Works as evidential fruit, never legal ground

After a sinner is declared righteous, good works arise not to earn approval but to bear witness to the reality of that verdict. Scripture uses agricultural metaphors—good trees bear good fruit—to illustrate how genuine justification leads to tangible acts of righteousness (Matt 7:17–20). These works include mercy, compassion, and integrity in daily life, the outward evidence of an inward change wrought by grace. They serve as public testimony to the transforming power of the gospel, attracting observers to the source of renewal rather than to human achievement. Importantly, works do not contribute to the believer's standing before God; they are rather the necessary outflow of union with Christ. When believers labor in acts of service, justice, and generosity, they do so out of gratitude for their acquittal, not to secure favor. The apostle Paul affirms that works prepared beforehand by God equip us to walk in them (Eph 2:10), underscoring that our obedience is itself a gift of grace. Any attempt to present works as legal grounds for justification undermines the gospel's core. Instead, recognizing works as evidence preserves the purity of both justification by faith and sanctification by the Spirit.

4.5.3 Final judgment "according to works" and the vindication of faith

Though justification secures our status before God, Scripture also teaches that believers will stand before the judgment seat of Christ to give account for their deeds (Rom 2:6–8; 2 Cor 5:10). This event—distinct from condemnation—evaluates the quality of each individual's obedience and rewards faithfulness. Works become the basis for receiving crowns and commendation, not for acquiring salvation itself. The judgment seat thus vindicates the authenticity of saving faith, demonstrating that a faith that justifies is one that has borne fruit worthy of its calling. Believers who have labored in love and served in humility will hear "Well done, good and faithful servant," a recognition that validates both the believer's efforts and God's grace (Matt 25:21). Conversely, those whose lives exhibit little evidence of transformation may suffer loss of reward, though they remain secure in Christ's verdict. This future reckoning underscores the seriousness with which God regards obedience, while simultaneously affirming that works serve a distinct purpose from the ground of justification. Understanding this judgment as the culmination of sanctification motivates believers to live with eternity's perspective, knowing that every act of grace-empowered obedience will ultimately be honored.

Having seen how justification and obedience interrelate— grounded in faith yet demonstrated in works and ultimately vindicated in judgment—we turn next to the assurance that flows from the believer's once-for-all verdict.

4.6 Assurance Flowing from the Verdict

4.6.1 Objective certainty in Christ's finished work

One of justification's greatest gifts is the objective certainty it provides: believers rest not on fluctuating feelings but on the unchangeable fact of Christ's accomplished redemption. The apostle Paul emphasizes that there is now "no condemnation for those who are in Christ Jesus" (Rom 8:1), an unassailable declaration rooted in the irrevocable nature of Christ's atoning sacrifice. This certainty transcends personal sanctification; it is anchored in decisions made in heaven's council and executed on Golgotha's hill. Since justification occurs in the courtroom of God and not in our subjective experience, believers can possess assurance even in seasons of doubt or dryness. The believer is thus invited to look away from self-examination and fix eyes on Christ's perfect merits, knowing that His work cannot be undone by human frailty. This objective foundation for assurance distinguishes the Christian hope from mere optimism, grounding confidence in divine promise rather than personal performance.

4.6.2 The Spirit's inward witness and sealing

While objective certainty anchors us, the Spirit provides an inward testimony that ratifies our justified status. Paul states that the Spirit "testifies with our spirit that we are God's children" (Rom 8:16), giving believers a personal sense of adoption and belonging. This witness is not a mystical feeling divorced from truth but an affirmation of God's Word working in the heart. Furthermore, the Spirit's seal marks us as belonging to the day of redemption (Eph 1:13–14), ensuring that nothing, not even our own doubts, can sever the divine guarantee. The inward witness works alongside objective certainties, providing experiential confirmation that God's verdict has reached our souls. Pastors and teachers historically have called this the Spirit's "testimony of adoption," an affectionate assurance that complements Scripture's declarations. Because the sealing is permanent, believers can find comfort even when tempted to question their status. The Spirit's continuous presence assures us that our justification is not merely declared but also applied and retained.

4.6.3 Pastoral counsel for seasons of doubt and spiritual dryness

Despite justification's objective and subjective assurances, believers sometimes encounter seasons of doubt, guilt, or spiritual aridity. In these times, pastoral counsel becomes vital, pointing doubting souls back to the certainty of Christ's work rather than to their fleeting emotions. The psalmist's honest lament—"Why are you cast down, O my soul?"— models a theology of divine dialogue that moves from despair to hope (Ps 42). Pastoral care encourages the use of means of grace—Scripture meditation, prayer, and fellowship—to rebuild assurance by rehearing the gospel. Counselors remind believers that doubts do not disqualify them from justification; rather, they highlight the need to reengage with the objective grounds of salvation. Churches have long practiced "spiritual direction," guiding individuals to revisit baptismal vows and communion's remembrance of the Lord's death. In this way, pastoral ministry becomes a conduit of grace, helping churches sustain confidence through the valleys of spiritual life.

With assurance established through both divine decree and Spirit-wrought testimony, we next explore how the doctrine of justification has been received and debated throughout church history, shaping contemporary faith.

4.7 Historical Trajectories & Contemporary Debates

4.7.1 Early-church perspectives on grace and merit

In the post-apostolic era, church fathers such as Irenaeus and Augustine grappled with the relationship between God's grace and human cooperation. Irenaeus emphasized Christ's recapitulation of human history, underscoring salvation as God's unilateral work through the Second Adam. Augustine later contended that even the initial stirrings of faith are gifts of prevenient grace, countering Pelagian assertions of human ability to initiate salvation. His debates against Pelagius crystallized the view that merit resides not in human effort but in divine favor. Yet Augustine also affirmed the necessity of moral response, insisting that virtues borne in the believer's life demonstrate grace's fruit. These early controversies set the trajectory for understanding justification as an act of unmerited favor, while still upholding the genuine transformation grace produces. The patristic consensus thus laid the groundwork for later doctrinal precision, even as nuances regarding the interplay of grace and free will continued to be refined.

4.7.2 Reformation flashpoints: Luther, Calvin, and Trent

The sixteenth-century Reformation brought justification's doctrine to the forefront, as Martin Luther's discovery of "the righteousness of God" reignited debate over faith and works. Luther's insistence on sola fide confronted medieval theology's compromise of grace with sacramental merit. John Calvin elaborated a careful doctrine of imputation and union with Christ, systematizing how justification and sanctification relate. In response, the Council of Trent anathematized the Reformers' positions, affirming that works performed in grace contribute to one's righteous standing. These flashpoints forged enduring confessional lines, shaping both Protestant and Catholic identities. Yet both traditions affirm that saving grace originates in God's initiative, even as they diverge on the role of human cooperation. The Reformation thus sharpened the church's articulation of justification, highlighting its centrality for both personal faith and ecclesial communion.

4.7.3 The New Perspective on Paul and recent evangelical responses

In the late twentieth century, scholars associated with the "New Perspective on Paul" challenged traditional interpretations of Paul's critique of "works of the law," arguing that first-century Judaism understood covenant keeping differently. They suggest that Paul's concern was more about ethnic boundary-markers than legalism per se. Evangelical scholars have responded by refining the nuances of imputation and emphasizing Paul's holistic contest with both ethnocentrism and merit theology. Recent dialogues have enriched understanding of justification's communal and covenantal dimensions, while reaffirming its forensic core. These contemporary debates demonstrate that justification remains a vibrant locus of theological reflection and that every generation must reexamine ancient texts in light of fresh insights. Such conversations ultimately serve to deepen the church's grasp of how God declares sinners righteous in Christ.

Having charted justification's reception from the early church through contemporary scholarship, we now consider how the once-for-all verdict shapes everyday life and mission.

4.8 Pastoral & Missional Implications of Being "Saved Once"

4.8.1 Freedom from guilt fostering joyful worship

When believers rest in the certainty of justification, the burden of guilt lifts and worship becomes a spontaneous outpouring of gratitude. No longer preoccupied with self-condemnation, they can approach God's throne with confidence, offering lives marked by delight rather than dread (Heb 10:22). This freedom nurtures corporate worship that transcends formality, as communities unite in heartfelt praise for the Savior's work. Joyful worship also becomes a testimony to the watching world, illustrating how grace transforms shame into celebration. In personal devotions, the justified heart finds new energy to meditate on divine attributes, secure in the knowledge that acceptance is settled. Such worship, rooted in completed justification, heralds the gospel more powerfully than any sermon, drawing seekers to the source of unfettered joy.

4.8.2 Motivation for holiness rooted in gratitude, not fear

While fear of punishment might spur outward conformity, gratitude for justification cultivates genuine holiness from the heart. Believers, overwhelmed by mercy, pursue Christlikeness not to earn favor but to express thankfulness for a standing already secured. This gratitude-driven obedience produces a sustainable zeal for righteousness, as it rests on love rather than on dread of condemnation. Paul exhorts believers to present their bodies as living sacrifices, a rational response to the mercies of God (Rom 12:1). When holiness flows from grace received, it avoids the legalistic pitfalls of performance-based religion. Instead, it embodies the gospel's liberating power, inviting others to experience freedom from fear through Christ.

4.8.3 Fuel for justice, compassion, and peacemaking in a fractured world

Justification by faith carries profound social implications, propelling believers into service for the marginalized with gospel zeal. Secure in God's verdict, they are free to devote resources and energy to justice initiatives, mercy ministries, and reconciliation efforts without ulterior motives. The doctrine's emphasis on imputed righteousness also guards against self-righteous activism, reminding workers that any good they do is itself a grace-enabled fruit. Motivated by Christ's love, restored communities span ethnic, economic, and cultural divides, embodying the reconciled reality of God's kingdom. As ambassadors of grace, justified believers engage broken systems—poverty, prejudice, and violence—urging transformation not by coercion but by incarnational witness. This missional outworking demonstrates that a salvation once and for all empowers the church to address both spiritual and social ruin with compassion and courage.

Conclusion

Having unpacked the doctrine of justification, we see that salvation's legal heart is a gracious verdict pronounced by God and received through faith alone. This once-for-all declaration transforms the believer's identity, liberating from guilt and empowering a life of joyful obedience. Historical debates and pastoral challenges may cloud our understanding, but the core truth remains unchanged: Christ's righteousness becomes ours the moment we trust in Him. As we leave this courtroom behind, we carry forward a liberty that fuels worship, service, and mission, confident that the One who justified will also carry us safely to the day of final vindication. With this firm foundation established, we now turn to the lived reality of new birth and adoption—how sinners move from legal pardon into vibrant, relational life in God's family.

Chapter 5. Conversion Experienced and Assured

Justification settles the believer's legal standing once for all, yet salvation is not fully appreciated until that judicial decree is felt, confessed, and lived out in real time. Conversion is Scripture's term for this personal awakening – the moment when the Spirit's internal summons breaks through spiritual deadness, redirects the heart toward Christ, and launches a lifetime of grateful obedience. Historically the church has described conversion as a decisive turning: from darkness to light, from idols to the living God, from self-reliance to whole-souled dependence on the crucified and risen Lord (Acts 26:18; 1 Thess 1:9). Although the inner work of grace is invisible, it produces unmistakable outward signs: a new hunger for truth, a renunciation of cherished sins, and a public confession that Jesus is Lord. This chapter traces that transformative encounter from first conviction to settled assurance, showing how the same Spirit who opened blind eyes also sustains faith through trials, restores the fallen, and propels the converted into mission. Our concern is neither emotional enthusiasm nor bare intellectual assent, but the

Spirit-wrought change that knits the justified sinner into Christ's living body and secures the soul against every storm (John 3:8; Rom 8:16).

5.1 Awakening: Spirit-Wrought Conviction and the Gospel Call

5.1.1 Effectual drawing versus general invitation

Every presentation of the gospel extends a genuine invitation, yet only the Spirit's secret work transforms that external plea into an inward pull that the sinner cannot finally resist (John 6:44). The general call may reach countless ears through sermons, tracts, or casual conversations, but without effectual drawing it remains intellectually interesting or politely dismissed. Effectual grace, by contrast, penetrates native hostility, lowering entrenched defenses and implanting a desire the hearer never imagined. This drawing is neither coercive nor mechanical; it woos the will by unveiling Christ's surpassing worth so compellingly that refusal would contradict the awakened affections. Its power lies not in louder rhetoric but in the quiet authority of the Spirit who applies redemption sovereignly, yet without violating personality. As the heart is lured toward the Savior, the sinner begins to regard former confidences—achievement, morality, or indifference—as brittle reeds unable to bear eternal weight. Reordered affections then spur the mind to reevaluate long-held assumptions, triggering a chain reaction of questions about truth, purpose, and destiny. This inner magnetism explains why two listeners can sit under the same gospel and react so differently, one unmoved, the other pierced to the core. The Spirit's drawing also overcomes cultural or intellectual roadblocks, translating the timeless message into the hearer's native categories while guarding its purity. Far from bypassing reason, effectual grace grants new capacity to see Christ's glory as reasonable, satisfying both head and heart. Because the divine summons is rooted in eternal love, it never fails to reach its appointed object, though the timing may confound onlookers. The result is a God-centered conversion in which boasting is silenced and gratitude blooms. This hidden but decisive pull initiates the entire conversion sequence and sets the stage for Spirit-wrought conviction, the next movement in the awakening process.

5.1.2 Conviction of sin, righteousness, and judgment

Once drawn, the sinner confronts a threefold revelation the Spirit faithfully provides: personal sinfulness, Christ's perfect righteousness, and the certainty of looming judgment (John 16:8–11). Conviction begins when divine light exposes the heart's secret chambers, revealing not isolated missteps but a pervasive posture of rebellion. The awakened conscience recoils at habits once cherished, sensing a moral weight that worldly psychology can neither explain nor relieve. Simultaneously, the spotless obedience of Jesus rises before the mind's eye as the only standard that satisfies God's law, intensifying awareness of personal shortfall. Judgment then appears not as abstract doctrine but impending reality; the soul feels suspended over an abyss whose depth it finally acknowledges. This conviction is painful yet profoundly hopeful, for the same Spirit who wounds also points to the remedy He has provided. He prevents despair by illumining the cross as the intersection where guilt meets grace, showing that the Judge has supplied the Substitute. Conviction's purpose is therefore therapeutic, breaking hard soil so gospel seed can take root. It dismantles every excuse—cultural conditioning, comparative morality, religious pedigree—and lays the sinner naked before omniscient holiness. Though unpleasant, this moment is a mercy, for only the convicted soul can appreciate the beauty of pardon. Deep conviction also inoculates converts against shallow profession, ensuring that subsequent faith rests on honest appraisal of sin. Having thus confronted divine indictment, the sinner is poised to hear the gospel word with new ears, a dynamic explored in the ministry of the Word.

5.1.3 The ministry of the Word as catalytic spark

The Spirit ordinarily wields Scripture as His sharpest instrument, coupling divine truth with awakened conscience to ignite saving faith (Rom 10:17). Whether read privately, preached publicly, or recalled from childhood memory, the Word carries living power that surpasses human eloquence. Its narratives disclose God's redemptive storyline, situating personal crisis within cosmic rescue; its commands expose ethical bankruptcy; its promises unveil a righteousness received, not earned. As the Word is heard, the Spirit personalizes its message, shifting verbs from third-person observations to second-person address, until "Christ died for sinners" becomes "Christ died for me." The Bible's simplicity disarms sophisticated objections, while its depth sustains the most penetrating inquiry, making it the ideal tool for souls in transition. Embedded references to grace—"everyone who calls on the name of the Lord will be saved"—begin to sparkle with urgency once conviction has ploughed the heart. At this juncture the Word becomes both mirror and window: mirror reflecting sin's disfigurement, window opening onto vistas of mercy. Its double-edged edge comforts and confronts, insisting that rescue is free yet costly, gracious yet demanding full surrender. The catalytic encounter with Scripture culminates as the hearer crosses the line from consideration to commitment, turning to God in repentance and faith.

A soul thus awakened by effectual drawing, conviction, and the living Word is ready for the decisive turn described in our next section on repentance and saving faith.

5.2 Turning to God: Repentance and Saving Faith

5.2.1 Repentance defined—mind, heart, will redirected

Repentance is far more than regret; it is a Spirit-enabled reorientation of the entire person that regards sin from God's vantage and chooses a new path (Acts 20:21). Intellectually, repentance acknowledges the accuracy of God's indictment, agreeing that the wages of sin is death and that every defense is void. Emotionally, it produces godly sorrow, not self-pity but genuine grief for offending divine majesty (2 Cor 7:10). Volitionally, it issues in decisive action—a pivot away from cherished idols toward humble submission to Christ's authority. This movement is not a one-time apology but the inauguration of a lifestyle that keeps short accounts with God, confessing promptly and forsaking resolutely. Because repentance is granted by God, it never rests in vague intentions; it yields observable change such as restitution, reconciliation, and restructuring of priorities. Yet repentance remains gospel-centered, steering clear of morbid introspection by fixing hope on the Redeemer who welcomes broken spirits. The penitent discovers that righteousness is not earned through penance but received through faith, which naturally joins repentance as its counterpart.

5.2.2 Faith as personal reliance on the risen Christ

Saving faith rises when the convicted and repentant heart entrusts itself wholly to the crucified and resurrected Lord, relying on His merit alone for acceptance (Rom 10:9–10). It is a transfer of trust—from self to Savior—sealed by confession that Jesus is Lord and belief that God raised Him from the dead. Faith embraces Christ in all His offices: Prophet who reveals truth, Priest who atones, King who rules. This reliance is not blind leap but calculated confidence grounded in historical fact and Spirit-borne assurance. It appropriates the promise that whoever believes shall not perish, taking God at His word despite lingering questions. Faith thus unites the soul to Christ, enabling immediate participation in His righteousness and life. The believer rests, yet that rest energizes obedience, illustrating how faith and repentance form two inseparable facets of the same conversion gem.

5.2.3 The simultaneity of turning from idols and turning toward God

Biblical conversion always involves a twofold movement: repudiating false gods and embracing the true (1 Thess 1:9). These motions occur in the same Spirit-breathed instant, for one cannot cling to both Christ and competing allegiances. Idols may be overt—money, power, sensuality—or subtle—reputation, security, even religious performance. Whatever their form, they must be abandoned as empty cisterns incapable of quenching thirst. Turning toward God, the convert discovers a fountain of living water whose supply never fails.

This new allegiance permeates daily decisions, reshaping how time, talent, and treasure are stewarded. Persistent idol-exposure and renewal of faith mark healthy Christian growth, but the decisive break occurs at conversion, establishing the trajectory of the soul's journey. In that pivotal moment, allegiance shifts, and a new center of gravity stabilizes the heart.

The inward turn of repentance and faith seeks outward expression, which finds its first tangible form in confession, baptism, and entry into Christ's community, the focus of our next section.

5.3 Public Identification: Confession, Baptism, and Community Entry

5.3.1 Verbal confession—owning Christ before people

Conversion is personal but never private; Jesus insists that disciples confess Him openly, acknowledging His lordship before a watching world (Matt 10:32). Verbal confession crystallizes inner faith into audible allegiance, binding the tongue to the heart's new loyalty. Early Christians declared "Jesus is Lord" in defiance of imperial claims, demonstrating that confession can carry weighty cost. Today, confession may occur during baptismal testimony, workplace witness, or family conversation, but its substance remains the same: affirming Christ's deity, death, and resurrection as the sole basis for hope. This verbal profession comforts believers with the resonance of shared truth, forging solidarity with others who confess the same gospel. It also warns against clandestine Christianity, for silence about the Savior contradicts conversion's outward impulse.

5.3.2 Baptism as sign of union and pledge of a good conscience

Following confession, baptism provides the God-ordained sign of union with Christ, dramatizing death to sin and resurrection to new life (Rom 6:3-4). Immersion—or effusion where immersion is impossible—symbolizes burial with Christ beneath the waters and rising in His victory. Baptism does not effect salvation but seals it, giving believers a tangible marker of their transfer from darkness to kingdom light. Peter calls it a pledge of a good conscience, meaning it expresses inner cleansing and public commitment (1 Pet 3:21). In the act, the baptizand declares allegiance to Father, Son, and Spirit and is welcomed into the visible church. Because baptism is covenantal, it binds participants to mutual discipleship, inviting accountability and support from the community.

5.3.3 Incorporation into a covenant community with shared practices

Conversion blossoms within community, not isolation. The newly baptized join a fellowship devoted to apostolic teaching, shared meals, corporate prayer, and sacrificial generosity (Acts 2:41-47). This covenant family provides fertile soil for growth, supplying models of mature faith, avenues of service, and structures for mutual care. Spiritual gifts flourish in this context, demonstrating the Spirit's wisdom in distributing abilities that build up the body. Community also safeguards doctrine, ensuring converts remain anchored in truth amid cultural currents. Through ordinances, teaching, and discipline, the church bears collective witness that Jesus saves and sanctifies.

Having taken these public steps, the convert turns to cultivate inward evidences of new life—affections and behaviors that confirm the authenticity of the change—our next subject of exploration.

5.4 Evidences of New Life: Spiritual Affections and Moral Transformation

5.4.1 New appetite for Scripture and prayer

Regenerated hearts instinctively crave the pure milk of the Word, finding in Scripture nourishment the old nature ignored or despised (1 Pet 2:2). Devotional disciplines shift from duty to delight as passages once opaque burst with meaning. Prayer likewise transforms from rote recitation to intimate dialogue with the Father, prompted by the Spirit of adoption who teaches believers to cry, "Abba" (Rom 8:15). This appetite reveals supernatural origin, for no external pressure can sustain long-term devotion to an unseen God. Over time, biblical meditation shapes worldview, influencing decisions about work, relationships, and leisure. Prayer threads through the day, short petitions and spontaneous praise joining set times of intercession. Together, Word and prayer act as twin lungs through which the new creation breathes, sustaining spiritual vitality amid life's complexities.

5.4.2 Love for the brethren as family trait

A second evidence of conversion is sincere love for fellow believers, springing from shared union with Christ (1 John 3:14). This affection transcends natural affinity, linking diverse personalities through a blood-bought bond. Practical expressions include hospitality, financial assistance, and emotional support, each reflecting the Savior's sacrificial love. The family trait of love grows through conflict resolution and forgiveness, teaching patience and humility. As believers serve one another, outsiders observe that discipleship is more than private spirituality; it is embodied community. The presence of genuine affection affirms to the convert's own conscience that the Spirit has indeed implanted new life.

5.4.3 Fruit of the Spirit replacing works of the flesh

Conversion inaugurates a moral transformation as the Spirit cultivates love, joy, peace, patience, kindness, goodness, faithfulness, gentleness, and self-control (Gal 5:22-23). These virtues gradually displace envy, immorality, anger, and strife, evidencing sanctification's early bloom. Growth is neither instant nor uniform; setbacks occur, yet an unmistakable trajectory emerges toward Christlike character. Fellow believers encourage progress, celebrating victories and admonishing lapses. Even secular observers may notice the change, asking for the reason behind newfound composure or integrity, providing evangelistic opportunities. The fruit of the

Spirit also shapes corporate culture, producing congregations marked by grace rather than competition. As these evidences accumulate, assurance deepens, reinforcing the convert's confidence that the faith professed is indeed the faith possessed.

The emergence of new affections and behaviors naturally raises questions about stability: How can such transformation endure trials and failures? The following sections will explore assurance, perseverance, and restoration, showing how the God who began this good work will surely bring it to completion.

5.5 Assurance Anchored: Objective Grounds, Subjective Witness, Corporate Confirmation

5.5.1 Grounded in Christ's finished work and the Father's promises

The strongest pillar of Christian assurance is the unalterable reality that Christ's obedience and sacrifice have perfectly met every legal demand of God's law (Heb 6:17 – 19). Because the verdict of justification rests on deeds accomplished outside the believer—deeds that cannot be undone by time, temptation, or even death—confidence in salvation is ultimately a confidence in Christ Himself. The Father underscored this certainty with an oath, condescending to human frailty by swearing on His own character so that heirs of grace would possess "strong encouragement." Divine immutability means that the verdict delivered cannot be reversed by shifting moods in heaven or earth; it is as stable as the throne from which it was pronounced. Objective assurance is therefore historical and covenantal: it points to a cross planted in real soil, a tomb vacated on a real morning, and a Savior now enthroned at God's right hand. When consciences tremble, believers are exhorted to fix their gaze not on fluctuating moral performance but on the blood that speaks a better word than condemnation. The forensic nature of justification guarantees that no new evidence can arise to reopen the case; Christ has already shouldered every accusation. Even future sins, foreseen before the foundation of the world, were drawn into the reckoning of Calvary. Thus, assurance draws its first breath in the atmosphere of objective fact—unseen by the senses yet more certain than the rising sun. This certainty does not breed presumption; it breeds worship, for grace this secure compels humble awe. The believer's task is not to supplement the foundation but to remember it, preaching the gospel to oneself when fears whisper of divine displeasure. Objective assurance also nourishes churches, for a congregation confident in unshakable grace becomes a community marked by stability rather than anxiety. Saints who know they are loved to the uttermost can risk vulnerability, confess sin, and serve sacrificially, liberated from the need to earn divine favor. This objectivity thus prepares the heart to hear the Spirit's inner witness, enlarging assurance beyond legal categories into filial intimacy.

5.5.2 Spirit's testimony and the believer's conscience

While the finished work of Christ secures the legal basis of assurance, the Spirit of adoption presses that verdict into the believer's consciousness, creating an internal resonance that words alone cannot supply (Rom 8:15 – 16). He whispers sonship in the quiet recesses of the heart, teaching trembling souls to address the Almighty with the nearness of "Abba." This testimony is not a mystical voice detached from Scripture; it is the Spirit's illumination of gospel truths, causing them to glow with personal relevance. As the believer meditates on promises, the Spirit sparks conviction that these promises belong to *me*, not merely to an abstract category called the elect. Such assurance may surge during worship, surface in daily prayer, or dawn gradually like morning light, but its effect is recognizable peace that overrides accusations within and without. The Spirit's witness also calibrates the conscience, refusing to allow false security when sin is cherished, yet rushing comfort when sin is confessed and forsaken. He is both seal and guide: sealing the believer for the day of redemption and guiding obedience so assurance remains vibrant. Doubts can still arise—scripture records saints who questioned their standing—yet the Spirit never abandons His role as Comforter; He steadily steers them back to Christ's sufficiency. Spiritual disciplines such as Scripture meditation and corporate praise create arenas where His witness is most readily perceived. Even moments of suffering can amplify assurance, for the Spirit reminds believers that affliction confirms their sonship, echoing the experience of the Man of Sorrows. Thus, subjective witness harmonizes with objective fact, offering a stereophonic assurance that fills both head and heart. This inner certainty flourishes best, however, in the soil of healthy Christian fellowship, where the corporate body echoes and authenticates what the Spirit speaks privately.

5.5.3 Congregational affirmation through fellowship and discipline

God never intended conversion to be a solitary journey; assurance matures within the chorus of redeemed voices that form the local church (Heb 3:13; Matt 18:18). Fellow believers observe one another's lives, spotting evidences of grace that individuals, blinded by self-scrutiny, may overlook. Words like "Brother, I see the Spirit's patience shaping you" become Spirit-empowered echoes of heaven's verdict, reinforcing assurance through relational testimony. The ordinances likewise play a confirming role: the Lord's Supper re-preaches the gospel every time bread is broken and cup is shared, inviting participants to taste forgiveness. Corporate worship wraps individual hearts in congregational faith, reminding struggling saints that they are part of a family secured by the same blood. Discipline, too, though feared by some, functions as redemptive affirmation; when a church corrects lovingly, it declares that holiness matters because sonship is real. Even the rare act of excommunication aims at restoration, underlining the seriousness of covenant identity. Robust fellowship—marked by hospitality, prayer, and mutual service—creates a culture where doubts can be voiced without shame and answered with gospel truth. In small groups and informal conversations, seasoned believers lend perspective to the young in faith, sharing stories of God's sustaining grace through decades of trials. This multi-voiced assurance guards against the isolation that often magnifies doubt. Thus, corporate confirmation adds a communal dimension to assurance, completing the triad of objective, subjective, and communal grounds.

Having anchored assurance in Christ's work, the Spirit's witness, and the church's affirmation, we now turn to perseverance, examining how converts guard and grow this faith amid life's inevitable pressures.

5.6 Perseverance: Guarding Faith amid Temptation and Trial

5.6.1 Means of grace—Word, sacraments, prayer, fellowship

Perseverance is not spiritual autopilot; God ordains concrete channels—means of grace—through which He sustains faith (Acts 2:42). Consistent exposure to Scripture renews the mind, aligning desires with divine priorities and arming believers against deceptive philosophies. The sacraments visibly dramatize the gospel, sealing believers to the covenant and refreshing assurance each time they are received in faith. Prayer functions as relational oxygen, drawing strength from the throne of grace for timely help. Fellowship provides encouragement, accountability, and practical assistance, weaving individual strands into a rope strong enough to withstand persecution and pain. When these practices coalesce into a rhythm of life, believers are spiritually nourished, just as physical bodies thrive on balanced diet and exercise. Neglect of the means weakens resolve; wholehearted engagement fortifies perseverance. God's design is parental: He supplies the feast but bids children eat. Reliance on unusual experiences rather than ordinary means often breeds instability; scripture commends the steady plod of daily grace. Pastors feed the flock through faithful exposition, while the congregation responds in service and song, creating a cycle of giving and receiving that sustains the whole body. Perseverance, then, is communal as well as personal, flourishing where means of grace are honored and shared.

5.6.2 Spiritual warfare and armor of God

Christian pilgrimage unfolds on contested ground, requiring vigilance against an adversary intent on sabotaging faith (Eph 6:10 – 18). The armor metaphor underscores that gospel truths are both defensive and offensive equipment—belt of truth stabilizing, breastplate of righteousness guarding vital organs, shield of faith extinguishing fiery lies. Helmet of salvation protects the mind with assurance, while sword of the Spirit enables believers to counterattack with precise Scriptural promises. Prayer interlaces all pieces, maintaining communication with the Commander. Spiritual warfare is not sensational theatrics but sober resistance to schemes that would dilute devotion or distort doctrine. Temptations often masquerade as harmless diversions, unchecked bitterness, or glamorous shortcuts to influence. The disciplined application of armor dismantles these assaults, preserving loyalty to Christ. Victory in warfare reinforces perseverance, proving that divine strength is sufficient for every challenge. Defeat, when it occurs, drives believers back to the armory, reminding them that weapons must be put on daily, not stored as relics. A battle-ready community guards the weak, overlapping shields of faith to protect those momentarily faltering. Thus warfare becomes a collective endeavor, weaving perseverance into the fabric of shared struggle and triumph.

5.6.3 Divine preservation and human vigilance working together

Scripture presents perseverance as a dance of divine sovereignty and human responsibility, affirming in one breath that God will complete the work and in the next that believers must keep themselves in the love of God (Phil 2:12 – 13). Divine preservation provides the safety net; no sheep chosen by the Father and secured by the Son will finally perish. Human vigilance, however, keeps eyes fixed on the Shepherd, avoiding precipices that wound and entangle. This synergy is not a 50–50 partnership but a 100–100 reality: God supplies will and power, yet believers wholeheartedly engage. Perseverance therefore involves choices—daily repentance, disciplined focus, intentional community—that God empowers and rewards. Recognizing both elements prevents despair (as if everything depended on self) and apathy (as if nothing mattered). Trials become classrooms where divine faithfulness and human diligence cooperate, forging maturity. Over a lifetime, the believer can look back and see God's fingerprint on every rescue and their own footprints in every obedient step. This mystery inspires worship, not confusion, as saints marvel at grace that enables perseverance while crediting God with every ounce of endurance.

With perseverance mapped, we must address inevitable lapses: what happens when believers stumble seriously? The next section explores restoration, outlining God's gracious path for wandering saints back to fruitful assurance.

5.7 Restoration after Failure: Repentance, Discipline, and Renewal

5.7.1 The possibility of serious lapses in genuine believers

Scripture is candid about the frailty that lingers even in regenerate hearts; episodes like Peter's denial prove that true disciples can fall grievously (Luke 22:31 – 32). Such lapses do not annul justification, but they do disrupt fellowship, cloud assurance, and dishonor the Savior. Recognizing this possibility tempers triumphalism and fosters humility, reminding believers that vigilance remains essential. Serious sin often creeps in through subtle compromise, unconfessed bitterness, or prideful self-reliance—gradual leaks that sink ships if unaddressed. When failure erupts, shock can tempt saints either to despair or to minimize wrongdoing; neither response brings healing. Instead, grace invites honest acknowledgement, echoing David's unvarnished confession after his moral collapse. The Spirit's conviction may feel severe, but its aim is surgical removal of infection, not terminal condemnation. Jesus's prayer for Peter—"that your faith may not fail"—encourages every stumbling believer that intercession precedes repentance, ensuring ultimate recovery. Restoration thus begins with reawakened grief over sin coupled with fresh faith in Christ's advocacy. This realism regarding lapses protects the church from naiveté and prepares the way for redemptive discipline.

5.7.2 Church discipline as redemptive, not punitive

Biblical discipline operates like a shepherd's crook, designed to rescue sheep from ravines, not to bludgeon them (2 Cor 2:6 – 8). The process starts privately—one brother persuading another to reconsider destructive choices. If unheeded, others join, escalating love's effort to reclaim a wandering heart. Formal exclusion is a last resort, declaring that the person's profession no longer aligns with observable fruit, but even that severe step intends restoration. Paul urged the Corinthians to welcome back the repentant offender "lest he be overwhelmed by excessive sorrow," proving discipline's restorative aim. Properly applied, discipline displays God's holiness, warns the congregation, and demonstrates fierce commitment to each member's spiritual welfare. It tempers cheap grace, reminding all that Christ's blood was too precious to accommodate persistent rebellion. When restoration occurs, joy reverberates through the body, testifying to gospel power that heals broken testimony. Misapplied, discipline can wound deeply; hence leaders must administer it with tears, prayer, and unwavering adherence to Scripture's guidelines.

5.7.3 Ongoing confession and cleansing maintaining fellowship

Beyond crisis moments, daily confession keeps relational channels clear, allowing fellowship with God to remain vibrant (1 John 1:7 – 9). Confession is agreement with God's perspective, naming sin without euphemism and trusting the promise of cleansing through Christ's blood. Regular self-examination under the Spirit's gentle searchlight prevents small sins from calcifying into hardened patterns. The practice also cultivates humility, reminding saints that grace continues to be needed long after conversion. As believers confess to one another, mutual support strengthens resistance to temptation, dismantling shame. Cleansing is not partial; God promises to purify from *all* unrighteousness, restoring joy and readiness for service. This cycle of confession and cleansing fuels renewal, sparking gratitude and deeper resolve to walk in the light. Over time, lapses decrease in frequency and intensity as habits of holiness take root. Yet even seasoned saints rely on this promise, illustrating lifelong dependence on the Savior's fountain.

Having restored fellowship, believers regain spiritual momentum and overflow toward others. The final section demonstrates how assured converts become conduits of grace through testimony, service, and disciple-multiplication.

5.8 Missional Overflow: Testimony, Service, and Multiplication

5.8.1 Personal witness fueled by gratitude

Conversion sparks an irrepressible desire to tell others what the Lord has done (Mark 5:19 – 20). Gratitude energizes evangelism, transforming timid personalities into bold heralds of grace. This testimony often begins in natural circles—family, friends, co-workers—where authenticity carries significant weight. Sharing need not be polished; sincerity and a changed life compel attention more than eloquence. Story bridges cultural gaps, connecting the gospel to shared human experiences of pain, hope, and searching. The witness also matures as believers learn to articulate the gospel clearly, answering questions with gentleness and respect. Obstacles such as fear of rejection shrink when weighed against joy that others might know eternal life. Even if response is hostile, the act of witness pleases God and strengthens the believer's own conviction. Daily habits—integrity at work, kindness to neighbors—extend verbal witness into visible demonstration. Thus testimony becomes a lifestyle, not an event, permeating mundane moments with eternal significance.

5.8.2 Good works as apologetic before the watching world

While words clarify the gospel, deeds embody its beauty (Matt 5:16). Acts of compassion toward the marginalized illustrate God's heart for justice, refuting caricatures of Christianity as other-worldly or indifferent. Serving meals, tutoring children, advocating for the oppressed—all become living parables of kingdom values. Good works performed without self-promotion shine all the brighter, prompting observers to ask about the hope within. Ethical consistency in business transactions challenges a culture accustomed to compromise, revealing an allegiance higher than profit. Generosity disrupts consumerist narratives, proving that treasure in heaven reshapes spending on earth. Together, these works compose an apologetic symphony, harmonizing with verbal proclamation and demonstrating that salvation renews whole lives, not merely private beliefs.

5.8.3 Disciple-making that reproduces the conversion cycle in others

The Great Commission calls every convert to participate in spiritual multiplication, teaching others to observe all Christ commanded (2 Tim 2:2). Disciple-making begins with intentional relationships, walking alongside newer believers through Scripture, prayer, and practical obedience. The aim is not information transfer alone but life transformation that equips disciples to disciple others. This cascading model ensures gospel advance without dependence on professional clergy, fulfilling God's design for a priesthood of all believers. Healthy disciple-making prioritizes character over charisma, depth over breadth, patience over hurried results. It celebrates progress, laments setbacks, and perseveres until learners themselves become co-laborers. When reproduction accelerates, communities experience exponential growth in both maturity and number, showcasing the Spirit's power at work. Ultimately, disciple-making loops back to awakening, as new believers confess faith, display evidence, secure assurance, and join the mission—thus perpetuating the glorious cycle of conversion experienced and assured.

Conclusion

Authentic conversion is more than a memorable prayer or an entry in a church ledger; it is the Spirit's ongoing testimony that the believer now lives in union with Christ. When conviction gives way to penitent faith, the verdict of justification becomes the believer's felt possession, confirmed by sacramental signs, nourished through fellowship, and authenticated by a pattern of growing holiness (1 Pet 2:2; Heb 10:24). Assurance thus rests on a three-fold cord: the finished work of the Son, the indwelling witness of the Spirit, and the affirming voice of a gospel-shaped community. Because that cord is forged by divine initiative, perseverance is ultimately secured by grace, even as believers actively engage the means God provides. From this place of settled confidence, the converted heart turns outward, eager to bear witness, serve the needy, and replicate the cycle of new birth in others (2 Cor 5:17–20). With the experiential dimensions of salvation firmly in view, we are now prepared to explore how grace continues its transforming work day by day in the long journey of sanctification—"being saved" in the nitty-gritty details of ordinary life.

Chapter 6. Being Saved Daily: Progressive Sanctification

The believer's journey does not end at the moment of justification but unfolds in a daily discipleship that renews heart, mind, and body by the power of the Spirit. Progressive sanctification is the Spirit's work of conforming us more and more to the likeness of Christ, transforming our patterns of thought, affections, and behavior to reflect the gospel's reality. This ongoing process engages every dimension of life— private devotion, public community, family relationships, workplace ethics, and responses to suffering—until the inner life and outer conduct bear the unmistakable marks of Christ. Far from a checklist of moral achievements, sanctification flows from union with Jesus, springs from gospel rhythms of Word and prayer, and is shaped by both ordinary disciplines and extraordinary trial. As the Spirit applies Christ's finished work day by day, believers discover that holiness is less a distant goal and more a present grace, empowering ever-deeper communion with God and increasingly vibrant witness to the world.

6.1 Grace-Based Foundations: Positional Identity & Progressive Reality

"Already holy" in Christ—positional sanctity

From the moment of justification, every believer is declared holy in God's sight—not by personal merit but by union with Christ, whose perfect life and sacrifice satisfy divine holiness on our behalf. This positional holiness is an irrevocable status reflecting the sinner's new identity in the risen Savior. Though inwardly imperfect, the justified Christian stands before the Father as if fully sanctified, because God has imputed Christ's righteousness to the believer's account. Such a declaration is not aspirational; it is a legal reality anchored in divine decree, assuring the believer that no condemnation can touch them. This grace-based foundation liberates from shame and fuels worship, for the forgiven cannot help but adore the One who has made them holy. Even when temptation reveals moral failures, the justified soul may stumble yet never falls beyond the bounds of divine acceptance. The concept of "already holy" precludes any competition between law-keeping and gospel-trust: identity in Christ precedes performance. Pastoral care repeatedly reminds struggling believers that positional sanctity is the ground of all other blessings—peace, hope, and purpose flow from this initial grace. Furthermore, this status shapes spiritual vision: rather than viewing holiness as distant achievement, the Christian sees it as present possession to be explored. Every spiritual discipline is thus undertaken not to gain acceptance but to enjoy and reflect the holiness already bestowed. Even corporate gatherings pulsate with this reality, as congregations affirm one another's status while exhorting to lived obedience. Recognizing positional sanctity prevents both despair and presumption, guiding hearts to rest in grace and labor in grateful response.

"Being made holy" day by day—progressive renewal

Though believers are already positionally holy, the Spirit continues to work within them, gradually conforming their character to Christ's likeness. This progressive renewal unfolds in the crucible of daily experiences—joy and sorrow, temptation and triumph—and is often imperceptible except in hindsight. The Spirit employs means such as Scripture, prayer, and fellowship to cultivate virtues and uproot sin, chiseling away patterns of selfishness and indifference. Day by day, the believer's mind is renewed, affections reordered, and will empowered to obey what once felt impossible. This process is neither uniform nor linear; seasons of rapid growth alternate with plateaus or even setbacks, yet the overall trajectory points toward increasing holiness. Just as a sculptor begins with rough stone and gradually reveals the form within, so the Spirit refines the believer through repeated encounters with grace. For some, transformation shows in gentler speech; for others, in sacrificial service or victories over besetting sins. Communities of faith supply encouragement and correction, reminding each member that progressive sanctification is both personal and communal. Patience becomes essential, as spiritual fruit ripens at different rates in different lives. The gospel sustains this patience by insisting that progress is never grounds for boasting but a cause for thanksgiving. As believers gaze on the unfolding work, they learn perseverance and deepen their trust in the Spirit's faithfulness.

Union with Christ as the wellspring of growth

Every stage of progressive sanctification flows from the believer's vital union with Christ, likened in Scripture to branches abiding in a vine. The moment a person trusts in Jesus, they participate in His life, drawing spiritual nourishment through constant connectivity. This union is dynamic: as Christ lives and loves through the branch, new shoots of virtue emerge where sterility once reigned. The Vine-Head supplies sap of grace—wisdom, strength, comfort—that sustains growth under every condition. Without this union, nothing good can be produced; efforts at morality become hollow and brittle. Believers maintain this union through dependence—prayer, listening, obedience— recognizing that even the smallest act of repentance or obedience reconnects a momentarily weakened branch. Divine pruning, though painful, serves this union by removing dead weight and directing resources toward fruitful areas.

Community life mirrors this reality, as local churches function like a vineyard, providing structure for branches to thrive in Christ's presence. When storms of doubt or trial assail, union with Christ anchors the soul, for His roots extend into the immovable knowledge of God's love. Thus, believers learn to abide, not as optional practice but as existential posture, breathing Christ's life into every moment.

Transitioning from the foundational realities of sanctified identity and union with Christ, we now examine the primary means by which the Spirit effects such transformation in everyday life.

6.2 Word & Prayer: Primary Means of Transformation

Renewing the mind through Scripture meditation

Sanctification begins in the mind, where Scripture serves as both mirror and map—reflecting the believer's true condition and charting the path of renewal. Regular meditation on God's Word aligns thought patterns with divine truth, exposing deceptive philosophies and rewriting internal narratives. As verses are pondered throughout the day—quiet fragments uttered while commuting, reforming mantras chanted during chores—the mind becomes a garden cultivated by grace. Repeated exposure to Christ-centered passages deepens convictions, shifts value systems, and equips believers to discern falsehood. This cognitive renewal shapes desires, for what one thinks about most deeply, one longs for most dearly. Old associations with sin loosen as new associations with holiness take root. Moreover, understanding Scripture in its narrative and doctrinal contexts prevents fragmentary readings, ensuring that isolated sentences serve the grand story of redemption. Group Bible studies and expository preaching reinforce private meditation, highlighting communal dimensions of truth. The renewed mind also controls speech and action, as thoughts inform choices. In this way, Scripture meditation becomes the centerpiece of progressive sanctity, transforming intellect and affections alike.

Praying in the Spirit—requests shaped by the Word

Prayer in the Spirit flows from a heart formed by Scripture, raising petitions that echo God's priorities and promises (Eph 6:18). The Spirit intercedes with groanings beyond words, aligning our imperfect requests with perfect will. Such prayer reflects sanctified desires: intercession for the lost, petitions for humility, and pleas for strength. Believers learn to pray Scripture back to God—praying the Psalms in moments of despair, echoing Epistles to petition for grace in trials. This Word-shaped prayer nurtures intimacy, forging a dynamic dialogue rather than monologue. As the Spirit highlights verses that address immediate needs—comfort in sorrow, courage in conflict—prayer becomes a living outworking of holiness. Habitual prayer guards the heart against anxiety and self-reliance, reminding the soul of its utter dependence. Corporate prayer meetings amplify this practice, weaving individual petitions into a tapestry of shared yearning. Over time, Spirit-led prayer cultivates patience, for answered prayers often unfold in God's timing, deepening trust. The synergy of Word and Spirit in prayer thus propels progressive sanctification, making the believer more like Christ in petition and praise.

Hearing, reading, studying, memorising, meditating—five disciplines of Bible intake

Five interlocking disciplines ensure Scripture saturates the believer's life: hearing in corporate worship, reading in private devotions, studying for depth, memorising for immediate recall, and meditating for personal application (Ps 1:2–3). Hearing engages communal faith, where expository preaching unpacks historical context and theological insight. Reading fosters individual rhythm, inviting fresh perspectives as the whole counsel of God passes before the soul. Studying employs tools—concordances, commentaries—to wrestle with nuances, cultivating conviction and doctrinal robustness. Memorising hides God's Word in the heart, arming the mind for temptation and enabling praise under duress. Meditation integrates these inputs, turning data into devotion. Together, these disciplines form a holistic matrix of Scripture intake that fuels transformation. The pattern invites both creativity and discipline, using journals, apps, or art to diversify engagement. Even as cultural forms shift, the underlying aim—Scripture shaping character—remains constant. Churches that emphasize all five disciplines equip members for sustained holiness. Over years, the cumulative effect produces a mind steeped in biblical worldview and a heart resistant to error. This comprehensive approach ensures that sanctification is not haphazard but systematically rooted in divine revelation.

By mastering these Word- and prayer-based disciplines, believers secure the wells from which all subsequent practices draw life. We now turn to the broader rhythms of grace embodied in classical and contemporary spiritual disciplines.

6.3 Rhythms of Grace: Classical & Contemporary Spiritual Disciplines

Solitude, silence, and Sabbath as antidotes to hurry

In a culture enamored with busyness, the ancient disciplines of solitude, silence, and Sabbath offer a countercultural stance that honors God's gift of rest (Mark 1:35). Solitude involves intentionally withdrawing from noise—technological or human—to meet the Savior alone. In that silence, the soul listens for God's voice, cultivates dependence, and discerns priorities. Sabbath extends solitude and silence into a weekly feast, ceasing from career demands, errands, and leisure distractions to celebrate creation's rest and redemption's promise. This rhythm refreshes body, mind, and spirit, reaffirming that worth lies not in productivity but in covenant relationship. Over time, these disciplines recalibrate tempo, teaching patience and presence. Even brief pockets of silence during a workday can prevent burnout and foster inner stillness. Congregations that model Sabbath and scheduled silence embolden individuals to resist societal pressure for constant achievement. These rhythms remind believers that holiness is a lifestyle, not a checklist—an ongoing posture of rest in grace that shapes identity and mission.

Fasting and generosity—retraining appetites and attachments

Fasting—abstaining from food or other comforts—reorients desires from creature to Creator, unveiling spiritual appetites that often masquerade as hunger. It primes the soul for deeper prayer, empathetic compassion for the poor, and renewed joy in God's provision (Matt 6:16–18). Alongside fasting, radical generosity challenges accumulation mindsets, teaching that stewardship involves releasing resources to meet others' needs (2 Cor 9:7). Both disciplines disrupt consumerist assumptions, forging habits of self-denial that cultivate Christlike compassion. Fasting clarifies what really sustains, and generosity declares trust in God's ongoing provision. These practices also foster solidarity with the vulnerable, as the privileged experience hunger or give material comfort. Over time, repeated cycles of fasting and generosity transform character, making the believer's wealth and health instruments of grace rather than idols. Congregational fasts and shared giving initiatives amplify these personal disciplines into collective witness. In an era of widening inequality, such rhythms proclaim the gospel's social implications, modeling a community that treasures divine provision and human flourishing equally.

Digital discernment—holy habits in an attention economy

Modern sanctification demands virtues for navigating screens, algorithms, and endless content. Digital discernment involves setting boundaries around technology use—designated "unplugged" times, app filters, and intentional media choices—to prevent mindless scrolling and spiritual distraction (Prov 4:23). It includes selecting edifying content, cultivating communities that encourage rather than exploit, and employing tools that limit access to harmful material. Believers practice "screen sabbaths," periods of total disengagement, to restore presence with God and others. Churches can equip members with resources on digital wellness, offering workshops on mindful media habits. Family rules regarding devices during meals, worship, and bedtime instill early habits of balance. Digital discernment thus becomes a modern spiritual discipline, guarding hearts against envy, anxiety, and comparison. As technology evolves, believers adapt discernment methods, ensuring that the Spirit's voice remains louder than any notification. In sum, cultivating holy digital habits secures the mind and heart for sustained sanctification in a wired world.

Having established core rhythms—classic and modern—that support transformation, we now address the critical practices of mortification and vivification that describe the inner mechanics of sanctification.

6.4 Mortification & Vivification: Putting Off and Putting On

Killing sin by the Spirit—mortification's logic

Mortification describes the Spirit-empowered work of putting to death the deeds of the flesh—those habitual thoughts, desires, and behaviors rooted in the old nature (Rom 8:13). This process begins with honest self-examination, inviting the Spirit to illuminate areas of concealment and denial. Once exposed, these sins are to be renounced decisively—"cut off your right hand" imagery signaling ruthless removal. Mortification is not ascetic self-help but a grace-wrought participation in Christ's death, for He has already broken sin's power. Tools such as confession, accountability partnerships, and confession of corporate vows aid this work. Progress results in diminished impulse toward former vices and growing sensitivity to the Spirit's promptings. Setbacks remind believers of their ongoing need for grace, leading to renewed dependence. Over the long haul, repeated acts of rebuke and refusal produce freedom, demonstrating that grace does not tolerate sin but empowers holiness. Communities that practice mutual mortification—lovingly confronting one another— advance this work in safe contexts. The logic of mortification underscores that sanctification is neither optional nor passive but an active collaboration with divine life.

Cultivating virtue—vivification's practice

Vivification complements mortification by describing the Spirit's enlivening of virtues that reflect Christ's character. As the old self dies, new appetites awaken—longing for truth, love for neighbor, and joy in righteousness (Col 3:12–14). Cultivating these virtues involves intentional habits: practicing patience in frustrating situations, responding with kindness to criticism, and choosing goodness in ambiguous moral landscapes. Scripture memorization furnishes promises that spur courage and compassion. Prayer petitions infuse zeal, while praise melodies foster joy. Corporate worship amplifies hope and unity. Over time, the consistent practice of virtue becomes reflexive, altering thought patterns and emotional responses. Spiritual mentors model these traits, providing living examples of vivification in action. Families that encourage kindness, perseverance, and self-control nurture these virtues across generations. Thus, vivification transforms the believer's moral ecosystem, replacing the barren soil of sin with the fruitful landscape of grace.

Daily repentance as lifestyle, not emergency brake

While mortification and vivification describe broad processes, daily repentance functions as the ongoing corrective that keeps the sanctified life on course (Rev 2:5). Rather than an occasional panic response to major sin, repentance is a habitual turning—an instant willingness to confess and realign with God's will. It involves noticing small deviations from Christ's example, confessing privately or corporately, and seeking restoration. A pastoral culture that normalizes confession and forgiveness prevents shame from stifling growth. Journaling sins and prayers encourages self-awareness and accountability. Small group check-ins foster honesty and support. This daily posture ensures that minor transgressions do not calcify into sinful patterns, maintaining intimacy with God and others. By making repentance a way of life, believers live in perpetual readiness for deeper transformation, discovering that grace meets every moment's need and supplies fresh cleansing.

As the processes of mortification and vivification stabilize, sanctified living extends into Spirit-filled obedience and the fruit of the Spirit, the subject of our next section.

6.5 Spirit-Filled Obedience & the Fruit of the Spirit

Walking by the Spirit versus gratifying the flesh

Progressive sanctification pivots on a choice of orientation: walking by the Spirit or gratifying the flesh (Gal 5:16–18). Walking by the Spirit involves moment-by-moment submission to His guidance, consciously choosing tasks, words, and attitudes in alignment with God's purposes. It requires sensitivity to promptings—compelling one toward kindness, caution, or courage—as the Spirit steers the believer away from fleshly indulgence. Gratifying the flesh, by contrast, yields to entrenched patterns of self-pleasure, power, or pretense, leading to guilt and distance from God. The spiritual dynamic resembles two overlapping circles: one of the Spirit's dynamic presence, one of the flesh's alluring but destructive forces. Believers learn to identify the lust patterns at play and rely on the Spirit's power to resist. Scripture, prayer, and community form tripwires that catch deviations before they escalate. As the Spirit's voice grows louder through habituated obedience, fleshly impulses lose their grip. Walking by the Spirit thus becomes the default as mortification and vivification bear fruit.

Nine-fold fruit as relational portrait of Christlikeness

Galatians lists nine attributes—love, joy, peace, patience, kindness, goodness, faithfulness, gentleness, and self-control—that collectively portrait Christ's character (Gal 5:22–23). These traits are not self-generated; they are the byproduct of Spirit-filled living, emerging naturally from union with Christ. Love grounds the rest, for loving obedience fuels patience and kindness, while faithfulness and self-control sustain promise-keeping and moral restraint. Joy and peace bubble up even amid trial, signaling an inner settlement in God's sovereign care. Gentleness tempers power with humility, while goodness demonstrates proactive benevolence. Taken together, this fruit evidences relational health—how a believer interacts with God, self, and neighbor. Communities that prioritize these virtues cultivate environments where spiritual gifts are deployed in harmony, not competition. Personal journals, small group reflections, and mentoring dialogues help believers monitor the unfolding fruit in their lives. Over years of Spirit-wrought cultivation, the fruit matures, transforming congregations into living testimonies of the gospel's power.

Joy-powered obedience: delight replacing duty

In Spirit-filled obedience, duty transforms into delight, for what was once onerous becomes a joyful surrender to the Lord's pleasure (Ps 40:8). The Christian does not obey out of slavish fear but out of affection for the One who first loved them. Delight in obedience arises as the Spirit renews affections; commandments begin to feel like invitations to deeper fellowship rather than burdensome rules. This shift produces resilience: joy-powered believers persevere under trial, fueled by the promise of greater glory. Practices such as gratitude journaling and celebrating small victories reinforce delight. Worship gatherings accentuate this joy, weaving testimony, music, and communion into experiences of divine gladness. As delight deepens, obedience becomes sustainable, even in seasons of hardship. The paradox of joyful obedience showcases grace: the yoke of Christ is easy, and His burden is light when carried in tandem with joy. This joy does not trivialize suffering but anchors the soul in transcendent hope.

Having examined how progressive sanctification unfolds through foundational identity, Word and prayer, daily rhythms, mortification and vivification, and Spirit-filled obedience, we now turn to the refining work of suffering and providence, which sharpen faith and deepen holiness.

6.6 Refinement through Suffering & Providence

6.6.1 Trials as crucibles for mature faith

Trials often arrive unannounced, yet Scripture assures believers that these pressures serve God's refining purposes (Jas 1:2–4). Facing hardship reveals the strength and depth of one's faith: untested trust may collapse under the first gust of adversity, whereas faith proven in the furnace emerges more resilient. In seasons of trial, the believer learns to rely not on personal resources but on divine sufficiency, echoing Paul's declaration that "when I am weak, then I am strong." This paradox becomes the anthem of sanctified living as believers discover hidden reserves of grace. Trials also expose idols—security, reputation, autonomy—forcing hearts to repent of misplaced trust. When circumstances strip away comforts, the soul confronts the question: "Can I still rejoice in the Lord?" The answer, over time, becomes a testimony to the Spirit's power, for joy surfaces even amid tears. Moreover, trials cultivate compassion: those refined by affliction become gentle guides to others in pain, reflecting Christ's empathy. Suffering teaches patience, the ability to endure unwanted delays without despair. It deepens prayer, as petitions shift from trivial requests to urgent pleas for God's nearness. Even unanswered prayers serve a purpose, training perseverance and reshaping expectations. Over the long haul, repeated trials solidify character, forging virtues that prosperity cannot produce. In this crucible, faith is not merely tested but transformed, integrating lived experience with gospel truth. As hope emerges from ashes, believers gain confidence that God uses hardship for ultimate good. Having seen how personal suffering refines holiness, we now turn to the broader shape of God's fatherly discipline.

6.6.2 God's fatherly discipline shaping holiness

God's discipline, likened to a loving parent's corrective hand, underscores His commitment to our maturity (Heb 12:5–11). Unlike punitive chastisement aimed at vengeance, divine discipline targets stubborn sin patterns, employing discomfort to draw us back to His heart. The tone is instructive rather than punitive: each setback becomes a lesson in humility, dependence, and obedience. Discipline may take the form of relational conflict, financial loss, or health trials, but its common thread is the Spirit's conviction that true holiness requires pruning. When believers resist His hand, discipline escalates in intensity—never to destruction but sufficient to capture attention. This grace-infused correction proves that we are God's children, not orphans abandoned in waywardness. It prevents the hardness of heart that emerges when unchecked prosperity breeds self-reliance. As we embrace discipline, our perspective shifts from seeing pain as random misfortune to recognizing it as purposeful instruction. Gratitude can even accompany discipline when viewed through the lens of divine love. Over time, God's training shapes priorities, aligning desires with kingdom values rather than fleeting pleasures. The faithful pastor speaks of discipline with compassion, helping congregants interpret suffering through God's fatherly care. In community, shared stories of discipline and restoration build empathy and encourage perseverance. Having considered God's sovereign use of suffering and discipline, we next explore how lament and hope function as twin supports during hardship.

6.6.3 Lament, hope, and resilience—forming a theology of pain

The biblical tradition of lament provides a structured pathway through suffering, modeling honest speech before God and anchoring hope amid despair (Ps 42; Rom 5:3–5). Lament begins in raw expression—tears, questions, cries of abandonment—yet it never ends in cynicism, for the psalmist pivots from complaint to confident expectation of God's deliverance. This movement from honest grief to hopeful trust forms resilience, a spiritual elasticity that prevents crises from permanently breaking the soul. Lament acknowledges the reality of pain without denying God's goodness, creating space for both sorrow and praise. In congregational worship, lamenting together fosters communal empathy and reminds believers that they are not alone in suffering. Pastoral guidance encourages journaling laments, teaching that recording prayers and God's responses fortifies memory for future trials. Hope, rooted in the resurrection and covenant promises, transforms lament into longing, expecting restoration and renewal. This dynamic nurtures spiritual resilience: even if joys are delayed, hope sustains a posture of trust. Over time, repeated cycles of lament and hope work like muscles, strengthening faith for the next trial. The theology of pain thus integrates truth and emotion, providing a robust framework for progressive sanctification. Having explored individual and communal responses to suffering, we transition to the ways the body of Christ cooperates in sanctification.

6.7 Corporate Sanctification: Fellowship, Accountability, & Mutual Edification

6.7.1 "One-another" commands as growth environment

The New Testament peppers its pages with "one-another" commands—love one another, encourage one another, bear one another's burdens—signaling that sanctification flourishes in community (Heb 10:24–25). These mutual exhortations create an environment where grace is both given and received, modeling the interdependence of the body of Christ. Love and encouragement spur obedience, for when a brother's faith shines in word and deed, it ignites desire to pursue holiness. Bearing burdens involves practical aid in times of need—financial, emotional, spiritual—demonstrating that grace encompasses tangible support. Forgiveness and reconciliation within the body prevent small conflicts from metastasizing into bitterness. The "one-another" ethos also guards against isolation, which often magnifies sin and stifles growth. Small groups and home fellowships provide intimate settings where believers can share struggles and victories. Corporate sanctification thus weaves individual trajectories into a tapestry of mutual transformation. Leaders model these behaviors, fostering cultures of transparency and compassion that accelerate spiritual maturation. As members invest in one another, they experience a foretaste of the unity and mutual love that characterize the new creation. Having seen how fellowship forges holiness, we now examine accountability and restoration.

6.7.2 Confession, counsel, and gentle restoration

Confession of sin to one another, coupled with godly counsel, operates as both a deterrent to hidden sin and a source of healing when failures occur (Gal 6:1–2; Jas 5:16). This practice acknowledges that sin festers in secrecy, but confession brings darkness into the light where grace operates. The act of admitting wrongdoing cultivates humility and frees the conscience from guilt's weight. Counsel by mature believers provides practical wisdom—scripture-based guidance on overcoming temptations, restructuring life rhythms, and cultivating spiritual disciplines. When saints gently restore one who stumbles, they mirror Christ's restorative love, affirming the repentant as fellow heirs rather than casting stones. Restoration is slower than rebuke, involving patience, accountability check-ins, and celebration when progress manifests. Communities that neglect confession and restoration risk moral inertia or cloistered perfectionism. By contrast, churches that practice transparent confession build deep trust, fostering an atmosphere where sanctification is communal work. This pattern transitions naturally into the diversity of gifts that equip the body for edification.

6.7.3 Diversity of gifts building a mature body

The Spirit dispenses varied gifts—teaching, exhortation, mercy, leadership—not to showcase individual prowess but to equip the entire body for maturity (Eph 4:11–16). Each gift contributes to the body's health: teachers anchor doctrine, exhorters spur perseverance, merciful servants soothe wounded hearts, while leaders coordinate vision and service. The presence of diverse ministries ensures that every aspect of sanctification receives attention. Without gifted teachers, believers drift into error; without merciful ministries, wounded survivors languish in isolation. Encouragers and leaders help implement spiritual disciplines and corporate practices, maintaining momentum. Gifts operate best in synergy—

teachers and exhorters collaborate in small groups; mercy ministers connect members with means of grace. Proper gift deployment requires discernment and humility, for no gift alone suffices. As the body learns to value each contribution, unity strengthens, and sanctification accelerates. Over time, a healthy body evidences equilibrium, where no gift dominates and every member shares responsibility for communal growth. This synergy transitions believers to see everyday life as the next arena for sanctifying witness.

6.8 Vocation, Work, and Everyday Witness

6.8.1 Sacred-secular integration—work as worship

Sanctification extends beyond church walls into the marketplace, for believers are called to view every vocation as an opportunity to glorify God (Col 3:23–24). Whether carpenter or cashier, engineer or educator, work becomes an act of worship when performed as service to Christ. This integration shatters the false sacred-secular dichotomy by honoring God in ethical excellence, creative innovation, and compassionate collaboration. Workers pray for co-workers, invite them to Scripture study, and demonstrate integrity in small transactions, revealing the gospel in daily conduct. Communities and families support one another's vocational calling, celebrating achievements as collective milestones. When employers adopt Christ-honoring policies, they extend sanctification to entire organizations. Sabbatical rhythms and sabbath observance within workplaces protect rest as holy space. Over time, workplaces become mission fields where progressive sanctification manifests in reliability, honesty, and collaborative generosity. This everyday witness readies hearts for deeper gospel engagement, naturally transitioning into stewardship of God's resources.

6.8.2 Stewardship of time, talents, and treasure

Holiness shapes how believers allocate life's primary resources: hours, abilities, and finances (1 Pet 4:10). Time stewardship involves prioritizing means of grace, meaningful relationships, and restful rhythms over endless activity or trivial pursuits. Talent stewardship emphasizes identifying spiritual gifts, developing God-given skills, and deploying them for kingdom purposes. Financial stewardship frames earnings as sacred trust, prompting generous giving and thoughtful investment in gospel endeavors. Stewardship practices—budgeting, sabbatical planning, volunteer coordination—structure lives around kingdom values. Covetousness is replaced by contentment, anxiety over scarcity by trust in divine provision. Churches equip members with teaching on stewardship, offering workshops and accountability groups. Generosity initiatives—benevolence funds, community projects—translate personal holiness into social impact. Over time, faithful stewardship models gospel economics, equipping communities to bless the vulnerable and expand mission. This stewardship ethos flows naturally into witnessing wherever God has placed the believer.

6.8.3 Missional presence in marketplace and neighbourhood

As progressive sanctification unfolds, believers discover that God's mission extends into everyday contexts—offices, schools, and neighbourhoods become platforms for gospel demonstration (Matt 5:13–16). Missional presence involves intentional acts of kindness: bringing meals to new parents, tutoring students after school, organizing community clean-ups, or offering professional expertise pro bono. These deeds create open doors for spiritual conversations, building credibility for verbal witness. Missional entrepreneurs integrate purpose and profit, launching ventures that reflect kingdom ethics and serve local needs. Digital platforms extend presence to online neighbourhoods, requiring the same grace and truth. Missional presence also means interceding for communities, praying for local leaders and economic renewal. As believers dwell in their cities and cultures, they embody the reconciliation between God and humanity, offering glimpses of the coming kingdom. Such incarnational ministry illustrates that sanctification is not private piety but a public testimony lived out in real places. From contexts of work and home, believers turn to the spiritual battlefield that awaits, explored in our next section.

6.9 Spiritual Warfare: Standing Firm & Advancing

6.9.1 Armor of God revisited—defensive postures

Sanctification includes readiness for spiritual conflict, necessitating the daily donning of divine armor described in Ephesians 6. The belt of truth secures the believer against deceptive philosophies, while the breastplate of righteousness protects the heart from shame and reproach. Shoes fitted with the gospel of peace enable faithful witness even when hostility arises. The shield of faith intercepts fiery darts of doubt—fears of failure, accusations of unworthiness—by deflecting them back to God's promises. The helmet of salvation guards the mind from confusion and despair, reminding the believer of assured destiny. Lastly, the sword of the Spirit—Scripture wielded in faith—allows for confident counterattacks against every lie. Practicing the armor involves daily intentionality, prayerful reflection on each piece, and memorization of corresponding verses. Churches can lead workshops on armor application, simulating scenarios for practice. Veterans of spiritual battle mentor novices in recognizing attack patterns. Over time, the body of Christ learns to move as an armed fellowship, securing both defense and direction in mission. Having reinforced defensive postures, we now explore offensive strategies.

6.9.2 Offensive prayer and Word-proclamation

Beyond defense, spiritual warfare calls believers to advance through strategic prayer and proclamation of Scripture (2 Cor 10:3–5). Offensive prayer intercepts evil schemes, requests the tearing down of strongholds, and petitions for the release of captive hearts. Corporate prayer gatherings for mission, revival, and justice launch assaults on darkness through united intercession. Word-proclamation—preaching, teaching, and personal testimony—exposes lies and establishes truth, breaking through spiritual barriers. Targeted declarations of gospel realities bring freedom to areas of oppression—addiction, inner torment, systemic injustice. Training sessions equip believers to engage in spiritual warfare prayer, emphasizing humility and dependence on the Spirit. Victory prayers often coincide with visible breakthroughs—recovered addicts, reconciled families, transformed communities. Such offensive application of the Word demonstrates sanctification's outward power and reinforces defensive postures. Having combined defense and offense, we next consider how discernment safeguards this warfare.

6.9.3 Discernment of schemes—truth versus deception

Successful warfare requires discernment, the ability to distinguish between divine promptings and demonic deceptions (1 Pet 5:8–9). Discernment grows from intimate knowledge of Scripture, sensitivity to the Spirit's voice, and communal counsel. False spirits masquerade as angels of light, offering counterfeit revelation, prosperity lies, or moral shortcuts. Believers learn to test every spirit against biblical criteria—Christ-exaltation, holiness, truthful fruit. Discernment also applies to ethical choices in technology, relationships, and leadership, exposing potential compromises. Regular practice—via case studies in small groups, prayerful reflection on inner convictions, and guidance from mature mentors—sharpens this capacity. Discernment protects sanctified living from subtle drift and equips the church to navigate complex cultural challenges. As warfare concludes with both defense and offense informed by discernment, believers stand ready for final hope. We now turn to the promise of glorification that fuels perseverance.

6.10 Hope-Fueled Perseverance & the Promise of Glorification

6.10.1 Fixing eyes on the appearing of Christ

Sanctification's ultimate motivation is the believer's anticipation of Christ's return, when the many facets of holiness will be perfected in a single glorious moment (1 John 3:2–3). Fixing one's eyes on that future appearing transforms present struggles into training grounds for eternal glory. The promise of transformation—mortality swallowed by immortality, weakness replaced by power—ignites perseverance under every trial. Corporate creeds and hymns that celebrate Christ's return reinforce this future focus, reminding believers that "we wait for new heavens and a new earth." This eschatological lens reorients time, making present sufferings light compared to the weight of glory to come. As hope anchors the soul, daily sanctification becomes not drudgery but a joyful preparation for an unblemished inheritance. Hope also fosters generosity, as believers recall that their treasures lie in heaven. With eyes fixed on the horizon, the Spirit empowers the final section on the guarantee of our journey's completion.

6.10.2 The Spirit's guarantee and longing for completion

The Spirit not only initiates sanctification but guarantees its consummation, serving as a deposit of the believer's coming inheritance (2 Cor 5:5). This down payment assures that every ounce of grace invested will yield full redemption of body and soul. By cultivating longing for completion, the Spirit stokes desire for holiness, impatience with half-measures, and audacity in prayer. Believers learn that present imperfections are temporary, driving them toward deeper reliance on divine power. This guarantee also sustains endurance, as doubts wane when the Spirit whispers of fulfilled promise. Congregational celebrations of confirmation, commissioning, and baptisms highlight the Spirit's ongoing guarantee and strengthen collective anticipation. Even amid discouragement, the Spirit's presence testifies that sanctification's finish line draws closer.

6.10.3 Finishing well—patterns for lifelong faithfulness

Finally, the tapestry of sanctification finds its design in patterns forged by those who finish well—Hebrews' "great cloud of witnesses" who endured to the end. Lifelong faithfulness involves periodic renewal: reaffirming conversion commitments, revisiting spiritual disciplines, and mentoring younger believers. It requires vigilance against complacency, recognizing that sanctification's journey ceases only at glorification. Practices such as annual retreats, spiritual biographies, and legacy projects help seasoned saints evaluate progress and chart new courses. Communities celebrate retirees' testimonies, acknowledging endurance as gospel fruit. Churches establish "finish-line ministries" for elders, equipping them to pass torches to new generations. As each believer runs the race with endurance, their faithful finish illuminates the path for others, embodying the promise that God who began a good work will complete it on the final day.

Conclusion

By God's design, the same grace that secured our justification propels our growth in Christlikeness, forging character in the crucible of spiritual disciplines, communal encouragement, and the fires of trial. Every act of obedience, from the simplest moment of prayer to the most sacrificial service, testifies to an inner reality that is being reshaped by divine life. This lifelong transformation anticipates the final redemption of our bodies at Christ's return, instilling hope that current struggles will yield eternal glory. As we press on in faith, the promise of ultimate glorification fuels perseverance, reminding us that "He who began a good work will bring it to completion" (Philippians 1:6). Thus, progressive sanctification becomes both the pathway of present joy and the preparation for future consummation, anchoring the believer in the assurance that each step toward holiness is guided and guaranteed by the faithful grace of God.

Chapter 7. Spirit-Empowered Living

No aspect of Christian life can flourish without the active presence of the Holy Spirit, whose power transforms believers from within and equips them for every good work. In the New Testament, Jesus promises a Comforter who will abide with His people, guiding them into truth, empowering them to witness boldly, and shaping their character to reflect the Savior's own likeness (John 14:16–17; Acts 1:8). Spirit-empowered living is not an optional extra but the very air that the baptized soul breathes—infusing prayer, worship, ministry, and even suffering with dynamic, divine energy. As the Spirit renews minds, ignites spiritual gifts, and fosters corporate unity, He knits individuals into a living temple where God's presence dwells. This chapter explores how the Spirit's indwelling presence moves beyond initial regeneration into ongoing filling, guidance, gifting, and sustaining power, ensuring that every dimension of life—personal devotion, communal worship, everyday work, and mission—bears the unmistakable signature of divine life at work.

7.1 Personhood & Deity of the Spirit

7.1.1 Eternal procession and Trinitarian equality

The Holy Spirit is not a force or impersonal power but the third Person of the Trinity, eternally proceeding from the Father and the Son in the divine life. His procession is an eternal reality, not a creation event, underscoring that He shares fully in the Godhead's uncreated, timeless being. Jesus spoke of sending the Spirit from the Father to be the believer's Advocate, indicating equality in purpose and essence with the other Persons (John 15:26). The Spirit's deity is affirmed when Peter equates Ananias lying to the Spirit with lying to God, a stark biblical affirmation of His divine status (Acts 5:3–4). Early church debates over Arianism hinged on understanding the Spirit's divinity, resolving that only a fully divine Spirit could effect genuine regeneration. The Spirit's eternal personhood means He knows, wills, and loves—and grieves—implying relational depth rather than mechanistic function (1 Cor 2:10–11). His involvement in creation, revelation, and redemption testifies to His co-equality and co-eternity with the Father and Son. Trinitarian worship thus includes the Spirit, for sacrificial praise is directed to "Father, Son, and Holy Spirit" as the one living God. Recognizing His personhood guards against reducing Him to a "power source" and invites personal communion through prayer and meditation. The Spirit's deity also undergirds every subsequent section of this chapter: only God Himself can indwell, guide, and empower the church from within.

7.1.2 Personal attributes—mind, will, emotions

Scripture attributes to the Spirit cognitive faculties: He searches the depths of God and reveals mysteries to believers, indicating a divine mind engaged in knowing and teaching (1 Cor 2:10–11). He manifests a will: He distributes spiritual gifts sovereignly to each member of the body as He chooses, showing personal volition (1 Cor 12:11). Emotions are likewise ascribed, for Paul warns believers not to grieve the Holy Spirit through sin, implying that He experiences deep sorrow when His work is resisted (Eph 4:30). Such attributes differentiate the Spirit from impersonal principles—He can be insulted, quenched, resisted, and obeyed, each response invoking relational dynamics rather than mere energetic function. The Spirit's emotions include delight in righteousness and horror at injustice, aligning Him with the Father's moral sensitivity. His will coordinates the global mission, sending workers and opening doors to unreached peoples. Believers learn His mood from Scripture: at Pentecost there is exhilaration, at Peter's preaching there is conviction, at Corinth there is mourning over division. Recognizing these personal traits invites believers to honor His inner life through worship, listening, and obedience, fostering intimacy rather than manipulation. This personal dimension sets the stage for understanding how He indwells and regenerates individuals, the focus of the next subsection.

7.1.3 Overview of Old- and New-Testament activity

From Genesis onward, the Spirit is active in creation, "hovering over the waters," shaping the formed earth with divine breath (Gen 1:2). In the Old Testament, He empowered judges, prophets, and artisans for specific tasks—raising Samson's strength, inspiring David's psalms, equipping Bezalel's craftsmanship—demonstrating selective filling rather than permanent indwelling. Prophetic messages flowed as the Spirit "came upon" individuals, enabling them to speak God's word with authority, yet could depart when unfaithfulness ensued. John the Baptist prophesied that Jesus would baptize with the Spirit and fire, predicting a new era of universal empowerment. With the Spirit's arrival at Pentecost, His mission expanded: He indwelt believers permanently, gifted the church corporately, and launched the global proclamation of Christ. New-Testament narratives record the Spirit's wind-and-fire descent, His anointing of Jesus at baptism, and His guiding the early church in mission. His activity transitions from selective empowerment of the elect in Israel to comprehensive indwelling of all who believe, signifying the inauguration of the new covenant. This sweep of Old- and New-Testament ministry frames the Spirit's enduring role in redemption's drama, leading us into a deeper look at His permanent indwelling.

 Having established who the Spirit is—fully divine, personal, and active throughout Scripture—we now examine how He takes residence within every believer as a seal of their adoption and a guarantee of glory.

7.2 Permanent Indwelling & Regenerative Presence

7.2.1 Spirit as seal of adoption

At the moment of conversion, the Spirit seals the believer, marking them as God's own in an irrevocable transaction (Eph 1:13–14). In ancient contexts, a seal signified ownership, authenticity, and protection; thus, the Spirit's sealing affirms both the believer's identity and security. This seal is neither superficial nor temporal—it places a divine guarantee on the inheritance of life, ensuring that nothing can annul the believer's status. The Spirit's seal also functions as a restraining barrier against final apostasy, testifying that every redeemed soul is inscribed in God's eternal ledger. Pastors assure wavering congregants by pointing to this seal, reminding them that salvation is not contingent on fluctuating experience but on the Spirit's abiding presence. The sealing by the Spirit also anticipates the full redemption of body and soul, anchoring hope in the promise of resurrection and glorification. In this way, the seal bridges present experience with future consummation, a connection we will revisit in the final chapter of this volume.

7.2.2 Temple imagery—believer and church as dwelling places

Scripture portrays both individual believers and the corporate church as temples where God's Spirit dwells (1 Cor 6:19; Eph 2:22). This imagery underscores that sanctified bodies and gathered assemblies are sacred spaces, consecrated by divine occupancy. In the Old Testament, the Spirit filled the tabernacle and Solomon's temple, validating those structures

116

as holy meeting places. In the New Testament, the Spirit's indwelling transforms every Christian into a living temple, inviting continuous worship and holy living. Corporate gatherings become new temples, a dwelling where every member contributes living stones to a spiritual house. Temple language shapes attitudes toward physical bodies: believers honor their bodies as sacred vessels, avoiding polluting behaviors. It also informs church order: gatherings are not secular meetings but sacred convocations where God's presence is both expected and revered. This temple reality frames every aspect of communal life—from prayer to discipline—as participation in divine residence. Recognizing the Spirit's indwelling raises the standard for individual and corporate holiness, transitioning into the subjective assurance this presence brings.

7.2.3 Security, intimacy, and assurance flowing from indwelling

The Spirit's permanent indwelling provides multifaceted blessing: security in salvation, intimacy in relationship, and assurance of God's ongoing care (Rom 8:15–17). Security stems from the seal that anchors the believer in divine custody, guaranteeing that no external or internal force can sever their bond with Christ. Intimacy arises as the Spirit aids prayer, empathy, and worship—enabling direct fellowship with Father, Son, and Spirit. Assurance flows from His witness within, testifying to the reality of adoption and empowering confidence during doubt. This trifecta fosters spiritual boldness, for believers act from the knowledge that God is present within them, guiding and sustaining every step. The Spirit's indwelling also equips for holiness: the same power that raised Jesus now empowers mortal flesh to obey divine commands. As intimacy deepens, prayer becomes more vibrant, worship more heartfelt, and obedience more joyful. Corporate life benefits as well—knowing that God's presence permeates every gathering inspires mutual respect and expectancy. Thus, the Spirit's indwelling presence serves as the bedrock for all subsequent fillings, guidance, and gifting.

With the Spirit firmly enthroned in every believer's heart, we turn to the dynamic reality of repeated filling—times when His fullness overflows into empowerment for service, witness, and joyful living.

7.3 Repeated Filling & Overflow

7.3.1 Commanded to be "continually filled"

Rather than a one-time experience, Spirit-filling is a continuous command, calling believers to be controlled by the Spirit's influence at every moment (Eph 5:18). The present-tense imperative suggests habitual or repeated action, akin to breathing: intake and release in a steady rhythm. This ongoing filling deepens our experience of Christ's life and empowers sustained obedience. It contrasts with occasional emotional highs, rooting sanctification in constant dependence rather than fleeting experiences. The command implies cooperative synergy: believers must yield daily, putting to death sin and opening hearts through prayer and worship. Regular filling prevents dryness and fuels mission, granting fresh boldness and fresh vision for God's kingdom. Churches structure spiritual retreats, worship nights, and prayer vigils to facilitate repeated infillings. Believers learn to recognize initial cues of emptied vessels—discouragement, distraction, defeat—and promptly return to the filling fountain. This pattern of seeking and receiving the Spirit's fullness forms the matrix for personal and corporate vitality.

7.3.2 Conditions for filling—yieldedness, faith, expectancy

Scripture links Spirit-filling to specific conditions: yieldedness of will, faith in God's promise, and expectancy of His generosity (Acts 4:31). Yieldedness involves surrendering personal agendas, confessing sin, and relinquishing control. Faith grasps the Father's promise to pour out His Spirit on those who ask, securing the right stance of trust. Expectancy readies the heart to receive, resisting the temptation to think Spirit-filling is reserved for an elite or confined to historical eras. When believers approach God with humble hearts and expectant minds, the Spirit finds open doors. These conditions mirror the posture of newborn infants anticipating nourishment, teaching dependence on divine supply. Over time, repeated experiences tighten the link between posture and promise, fostering spiritual sensitivity. Prayer meetings and sermon series on the Spirit emphasize these conditions, guiding congregations in practical application. When churches commit to modeling yieldedness, faith, and expectancy, they cultivate environments where Spirit-filling becomes normative rather than exceptional.

7.3.3 Evidences—joy, bold witness, grateful worship

The fruit of Spirit-filling manifests in observable ways: a buoyant joy that defies circumstances, courage in sharing the gospel, and heartfelt worship that radiates thankfulness (Gal 5:22; Acts 13:52). Joy surfaces as laughter, hope, and resilience even amid trials, signaling a deep wellspring of divine gladness. Bold witness overcomes fear of man, compelling believers to declare Christ to neighbors, colleagues, and strangers. Grateful worship spills into music, testimony, and generosity, as hearts awakened by grace overflow in praise. These evidences encourage others, validating the reality of the Spirit's presence. Churches often track qualitative changes—stories of joy, accounts of bold sharing, spontaneous outbursts of praise—as indicators of filling. Such markers reassure believers that the filling is authentic, not mere emotional hype. Over time, these evidences coalesce into an identity: a community known for joy, witness, and worship. This overflow then naturally transitions into Spirit-led guidance as the next major dimension of empowered living.

7.4 Guidance & Discernment in Everyday Decisions

7.4.1 Illuminating Scripture and conscience

The Spirit guides believers primarily by illuminating Scripture, unlocking fresh insight and personal application for life's decisions (John 16:13). Passages once read quickly gain new layers of meaning, highlighting specific next steps or attitudes to embrace. The Spirit also works through conscience, a God-given sense of moral sensitivity that signals right and wrong when informed by Scripture. When facing decisions— career moves, relational conflicts, financial choices—the believer consults the Word and listens for internal promptings. Prayer further clarifies direction, inviting the Spirit to confirm or correct initial inclinations. Churches reinforce this guidance model by encouraging Bible-based leadership and avoiding "magic-eight-ball" approaches to decision making. Over time, repeated cycles of Scripture-based discernment train the mind and conscience to function in harmony, reducing the sense of drift or confusion.

7.4.2 Inner witness versus external providence

While the Spirit speaks inwardly, God's providential workings in circumstances provide external confirmation of direction (Acts 16:6–10). For example, doors unexpectedly close or open, aligning with the Spirit's inner conviction. The missionary Paul experienced both inner prohibition and visible opportunity, using both to navigate God's plan. Believers learn to weigh internal witness and external providence together, neither elevating one exclusively nor discounting the other. Discerning patterns—synchronized prayers, timely resources, supportive counsel—validates the Spirit's leading. Conversely, overemphasizing providence without inner clarity can lead to misinterpretation of chance events as divine will. Churches teach members to test impressions against Scripture and seek communal counsel before acting on providential signals. This balanced approach guards against impulsive or paralyzed decision making. As believers grow in maturity, the interplay of inner witness and external providence becomes a reliable compass for personal and corporate mission.

7.4.3 Testing impressions—biblical, communal, missional filters

To avoid deception, every perceived leading must pass three filters: biblical alignment, communal affirmation, and mission focus (1 John 4:1). First, any prompting must accord with Scripture's character and commands; if it contradicts clear biblical teaching, it must be rejected. Second, the faith community—pastors, mentors, peers—confirms or questions discernment, preventing isolation and self-deception. Third, the proposed course must advance God's redemptive mission, avoiding purely personal agendas. These filters operate like a three-fold cord, strengthening discernment and preventing error. Case studies in small groups help believers practice applying these filters, cultivating wisdom for complex scenarios. Transitioning from personal discernment to Spirit-empowered gifting emerges naturally from a framework grounded in truth, community, and mission.

7.5 Charisms for Service & Mission

7.5.1 Diversity of gifts—motivational, manifestational, ministry

The early church recognized a wide array of spiritual gifts— motivational (apostles, prophets, evangelists), manifestational (tongues, healing, miracles), and ministry (teaching, helping, administration)—each serving the body's needs (Rom 12; 1 Cor 12; Eph 4). Motivational gifts chart vision and expand boundaries, stirring the church toward fresh expressions of mission. Manifestational gifts provide tangible signs that validate the gospel's power, stirring faith and compassion. Ministry gifts ensure that day-to-day operations—visitation, mercy, organization—are executed with care. This wide distribution prevents any single gift from monopolizing the church's focus, ensuring holistic health. Believers are encouraged to serve in areas where their gifts intersect with passion, maximizing kingdom impact. Over time, balanced gift deployment fosters synergy: prophets challenge us, teachers ground us, servers sustain us, and healers console us. Recognizing diversity of gifts also combats envy and discouragement, for each function is equally valuable in the body's growth.

7.5.2 Discovering and deploying gifts in love

While discovering gifts often involves personality inventories and pastoral insight, deployment requires concrete opportunities and feedback loops. Spiritual gifts become evident as believers step into service—leading a study group, praying for healing, mentoring a new convert—and observe fruit and affirmation. Love, as Paul insists, must govern all exercise of gifts, ensuring that ministry flows from genuine care rather than ambition (1 Cor 13). Accountability relationships help refine gift deployment, providing correction and encouragement. Churches create pipelines for training and placement, aligning individual gifting with congregational needs. Over time, deployed gifts become pathways for sanctification, as service challenges believers to rely on divine strength and cultivate Christlike character.

7.5.3 Safeguards against abuse—order, accountability, edification

Given the potential for misuse—overemphasis on spectacular gifts, spiritual pride, or doctrinal manipulation—Scripture outlines safeguards: orderly worship, mutual accountability, and prioritizing edification (1 Cor 14:26–33). Churches establish clear guidelines for prophetic words, healing ministries, and public prayers, subjecting all to pastoral and communal evaluation. Gifted individuals submit their words and methods to the leadership for discernment, ensuring nothing contradicts Scripture or love. Training in humility and servant-leadership protects against self-exaltation. Evaluating ministries by fruit—love, joy, peace—provides practical benchmarks. In this way, the Spirit's gifts flourish in healthy tension between freedom and structure, feeding both individual edification and corporate unity.

With a clear understanding of the Spirit's indwelling, filling, guidance, and gifting, we now turn to how He empowers believers to testify boldly, advancing the gospel across cultural boundaries.

7.6 Empowered Witness & Evangelistic Boldness

When the Spirit falls upon believers, He ignites a passion to proclaim Christ wherever they go, turning timid followers into courageous witnesses. The Day of Pentecost exemplifies this transformation: Peter, once silent and fearful, boldly declared Jesus' resurrection to thousands in the very city that crucified Him, resulting in three thousand conversions. This pattern repeats throughout Acts as the Spirit emboldens apostles and ordinary Christians alike to preach King Jesus in synagogues, marketplaces, and city streets. Spirit-empowered witness transcends personality types—it galvanizes introverts to speak up and gives extroverts a holy boldness tempered by love. Under the Spirit's influence, speech becomes seasoned with grace, words guided by wisdom rather than human rhetoric, captivating listeners with both clarity and conviction. Prayer often precedes these bold acts, as the church intercedes for Spirit-anointed opportunities and the courage to seize them. Missions teams report that Spirit-filled preparation in corporate prayer leads to unexpected open doors overseas, echoing the Macedonian call in Paul's vision. Even in hostile contexts, believers equipped by the Spirit share their testimonies with winsome vulnerability, inviting questions rather than demanding allegiance. Over time, communities see a steady trickle of questions, conversations, and conversions—evidence that Spirit-led witness is both reproducible and reliable. The Spirit also supplies language fluency or symbolic acts that resonate cross-culturally, bridging ethnic and linguistic divides. When opposition arises—legal threats, social ostracism, physical danger—the Spirit provides endurance and the words to speak at the right moment. Churches cultivate evangelistic training rooted in Scripture and Spirit, teaching how to depend on prompting rather than techniques. They celebrate stories of how the gospel advanced through Spirit-enabled steps of faith, reinforcing the expectancy that the Spirit will do likewise tomorrow. As these empowered witnesses multiply, they form networks of testimony that transform entire regions, turning the Spirit's initial descent into ongoing harvest.

Having explored how the Spirit empowers individual witness, we now turn to His role in igniting and sustaining corporate worship that renews congregations and sparks revival.

7.7 Worship & Corporate Renewal

Corporate worship under the Spirit's influence transcends programmed rituals, becoming a living encounter with God's presence that transforms both individuals and communities. In Scripture, the Spirit moves through song and proclamation: David's lyre calms Saul's tormented soul, and the early church's hymns reverberate with Pentecostal power. Spirit-led worship integrates ancient liturgy—Scripture readings, creedal affirmations—with spontaneous outbursts of praise, prophecy, or tongues, reflecting both continuity and innovation. This synergy of structure and freedom cultivates deep engagement, drawing hearts into awe and repentance. The Spirit often orchestrates corporate renewal through unexpected surges of conviction and unity, as when the Ephesians fell under Paul's preaching and burned their magic books. Such awakenings are marked by collective sorrow for sin, followed by communal celebration of grace. Leaders who depend on the Spirit resist attempts to manufacture experiences, instead creating space for the Spirit to breathe as He wills. They cultivate multi-sensory worship—music, art, drama, silent reflection—inviting diverse expressions of praise that resonate across generational and cultural lines. Prayer walks, fasting gatherings, and times of extended intercession become seasons of preparation for worship breakthroughs. Congregations learn to listen for the Spirit's cue, pausing mid-service for a word of prophecy or a moment of extended worship. Over time, these practices breed a culture of expectancy, where congregants anticipate the Spirit's movement rather than passively consume content. Historical revivals—such as the Azusa Street outpouring—offer case studies in how Spirit-driven worship can catalyze global movements. Today's churches draw lessons from these accounts, emphasizing humility, repentance, and social engagement alongside passionate praise. Through

Spirit-empowered worship, the corporate body experiences renewal that ripples into mission and societal transformation.

While corporate worship invites the Spirit's movement, certain attitudes and practices can grieve or quench Him; the next section examines these barriers and how to remove them.

7.8 Grieving, Quenching, & Resisting the Spirit— Barriers to Fullness

Even as the Spirit yearns to fill and guide, believers can grieve Him through sin and quench His fire through neglect, erecting barriers to empowered living. Grieving the Spirit involves personal sins such as bitterness, envy, and unconfessed anger—attitudes that wound His heart and stifle His work. Corporate dynamics also quench His movement: disunity, legalism, or cluttered agendas can suffocate the spontaneity He brings. When meetings prioritize human programs over Spirit-filled openness, congregations risk trading revival for routine. Ignoring gifts or dismissing prophetic words tightens the dam against His flow. Overemphasis on tradition without flexibility breeds a closed spine, deaf to fresh thunder of the Spirit. Resistance also takes the form of doubt—questioning whether God still moves through signs and wonders— effectively blunting expectancy. Breakthrough occurs when communities repent of these grieves and quenchers, confessing corporate idols and returning to simplicity of gospel dependence. Leaders then recalibrate priorities, carving out unprogrammed space for the Spirit's promptings. Personal restoration begins with confession and surrender, acknowledging that ongoing union requires daily re-submission. Small groups practice mutual accountability, identifying patterns that grieve or quench the Spirit and praying for restoration. As barriers fall, joy returns, creativity revives, and a fresh sense of the sacred permeates worship, ministry, and mission.

Liberated from these hindrances, believers can fully experience the Spirit's comfort and power, especially in times of suffering and weakness, the focus of our next section.

7.9 Comfort & Power in Suffering & Weakness

In life's darkest valleys—persecution, illness, loss—the Spirit functions as Comforter and source of supernatural strength, assuring believers of God's presence and enabling them to endure (John 14:16–17). His comfort goes beyond mere consolation; it infuses the soul with peace that surpasses understanding, anchoring faith in the midst of storms. When words fail, the Spirit intercedes with groans that articulate deep need, aligning human petition with God's will (Rom 8:26–27). This ministry enables believers to pray through pain rather than retreat into despair. The Spirit also imparts power to witness under duress, emboldening saints to testify even from prison cells or hospital beds. Physical weakness becomes a stage for the Spirit's glory, as demonstrated when Paul boasted in his infirmities so that Christ's power might rest on him (2 Cor 12:9). In communities facing communal tragedy—natural disaster, social upheaval—the Spirit rallies collective prayers, providing direction for relief and hope for renewal. He mobilizes resources through networks of compassionate believers, turning suffering into avenues for gospel demonstration. Seasonal lament is transformed into communal lament, where the Spirit knits wounded hearts together and reminds them that suffering is not meaningless but part of redemptive history. Over time, a theology of suffering emerges—one that refuses facile platitudes and embraces the Spirit's invitation to enter the fellowship of Christ's sufferings. As believers experience tangible deliverance or sustained grace under trial, their testimonies become powerful proclamations of Spirit-empowered living.

Anchored in the Spirit's comfort and strength, we now look ahead to how He serves as our guarantee of future glory, shaping our present hope and longing.

7.10 Eschatological Ministry—Firstfruits & Guarantee of Glory

7.10.1 Spirit as down-payment of future inheritance

Paul describes the Spirit's indwelling as a "firstfruits," a deposit guaranteeing the full redemption to come (2 Cor 1:22). Like the first portion of the harvest, the Spirit's presence signals that God's promises will be fulfilled without fail. This down-payment brings future realities into present experience: believers taste resurrection power and eternal fellowship even now. The Spirit assures that no trial or failure can nullify the inheritance awaiting God's children. This guarantee fuels worship and resilience, for every act of obedience engages not only time but eternity. Churches celebrate Spirit-baptisms, not as mere ceremonies but as visible pledges of coming consummation, bridging present sacrifice and future joy.

7.10.2 Transforming us from glory to glory—preview of glorification

As the Spirit works, He progressively conforms believers "from one degree of glory to another," foreshadowing the final glorification when bodies and souls are fully renewed (2 Cor 3:18). This ongoing transformation imparts glimpses of the resurrected life—moments of unshakeable peace, moral victories, and sacrificial love that exceed natural capacity. These "preview" experiences encourage perseverance, showing that the longings of the disembodied soul will one day find complete fulfillment. Spiritual disciplines and communal worship cultivate sensitivity to these flashes of glory, reinforcing faith. Personal testimonies of moral triumph or divine provision become evidence that the Spirit is already implementing the permanent realities of glorification.

7.10.3 Longing and hastening the Day—Spirit and Bride say "Come"

In the closing chapters of Revelation, both the Spirit and the Bride echo the prayer "Come, Lord Jesus," expressing a cosmic yearning for consummation (Rev 22:17). This corporate voice reflects an inner prompting, for the Spirit cultivates longing that fulfills sanctification's eschatological dimension. Believers live in "already" and "not yet," working for kingdom advance while yearning for the full manifestation of Christ's reign. This longing shapes mission urgency—"how can we delay when the harvest is great and the night is coming?"—and frames suffering as temporary shadows before eternal dawn. As the Spirit nurtures this eschatological hope, every prayer, act of service, and burst of praise becomes an invitation for Jesus to appear. Thus, Spirit-empowered living finds its ultimate purpose in hastening the Day when the Spirit's ministry will reach its pinnacle in glorification.

Conclusion

Spirit-empowered living reshapes the Christian journey from a self-driven quest into a Christ-enabled adventure of witness, worship, and transformation. The same Spirit who raised Jesus from the dead lives in each believer, guaranteeing that no obstacle—be it internal weakness, external persecution, or communal discord—can thwart God's unfolding purposes (Rom 8:11). As He distributes gifts, fuels prayer, guides decisions, and renews hearts, the Spirit forms a people ready for every good work and eager for the final consummation promised in glory. With eyes fixed on the Spirit's present power and future fullness, believers embrace a life marked by bold evangelism, sacrificial service, and resilient hope. The journey thus far brings us to the threshold of community expression and sacramental depth, where Spirit-wrought renewal manifests most visibly in Christ's body—the focus of the next chapter.

Chapter 8. Community and Sacrament: Corporate Dimensions of Salvation

Salvation's reach extends far beyond individual souls to the vibrant organism of the church, where believers share life, worship, and mission as one covenant family. In Scripture, God gathers a diverse multitude around Word and sacrament, forging unity out of diversity and forging a holy culture marked by love, accountability, and mutual care. Baptism and the Lord's Supper anchor this shared life in tangible symbols of union with Christ and with one another, while communal practices—fellowship meals, discipline, leadership, and worship—shape believers into a likeness of their Savior. This chapter explores how the corporate dimensions of salvation not only reflect the gospel's communal nature but also equip the church to embody God's kingdom in the world.

8.1 The Church as New-Covenant Community

8.1.1 Identity as the elect "people of God" and "royal priesthood"

The New Testament redefines the people of God not by ethnicity but by faith in Christ, calling all believers the "elect" who have been chosen before the foundation of the world. This election is not arbitrary favoritism but rooted in God's gracious purpose to gather worshipers from every tribe, tongue, and nation into one family. As recipients of divine mercy, believers are also declared a "royal priesthood," charged with offering spiritual sacrifices acceptable to God. This priestly identity entails both privilege and responsibility: drawing near to God in worship and drawing others into communion through intercession and proclamation. In Old-Testament shadows, Israel's priests mediated between God and the people; in the new covenant, every believer shares that mediatorial role, offering praise and prayer on behalf of the world. This corporate priesthood underscores the communal nature of salvation: no individual Christian stands alone before God. Instead, each is knitted into a body whose combined voices ascend as a fragrant offering. This collective identity also reframes suffering and joy, for personal trials become corporate opportunities for intercession and mutual comfort. Believers embody kingdom presence, modeling for the world what it means to be God's treasured possession. Understanding the church as God's elect royal priesthood impels every member to cultivate both intimacy with God and interdependence with one another.

8.1.2 Body of Christ—interdependence and diversity

Paul's metaphor of the church as the Body of Christ vividly captures both unity and diversity within the community of faith. Just as a human body consists of many parts—hands, eyes, feet—each with distinct functions yet indispensable to the whole, so the church comprises individuals gifted differently but united in one Spirit. No member may boast of superiority, for all parts share equal value in sustaining the life of the body.

The eye cannot say to the hand, "I have no need of you," nor can the foot say to the ear, "I can do without you," illustrating the mutual dependence required for healthy function. This interdependence extends beyond spiritual gifts to practical contributions: service, encouragement, teaching, giving, and mercy form an intricate network of grace. Diversity of ethnicity, culture, age, and background becomes a strength rather than a liability, enriching the body's witness to God's reconciling power. Tensions and conflicts inevitably arise, but the Spirit-given bond of peace calls believers to pursue unity through humility, forgiveness, and open communication. When one member suffers, all suffer; when one rejoices, all rejoice, modeling empathy and shared destiny. This dynamic unity amplifies the church's impact, as collective witness carries weight far beyond isolated efforts. Recognizing membership in the Body of Christ also nurtures accountability, for each person's actions affect the health of the whole.

8.1.3 Spirit-built temple—corporate dwelling place of God

The church is not only a body but also a dwelling place for God's Spirit, a spiritual temple under construction. In the Old Covenant, God's presence filled the tabernacle and temple; in the New Covenant, He indwells the gathered community, making every assembly sacred space. This temple imagery conveys holiness, permanence, and divine occupancy, reminding believers that worship gatherings are more than human conventions—they are entrances into God's manifest presence. The Spirit's activity within the corporate temple empowers worship, teaching, gift distribution, and mission, shaping communal rhythms around Word and sacrament. As living stones, individual believers find their identity in contributing to the structural integrity of this spiritual house. The foundation laid by apostles and prophets supports growth upward into a holy dwelling, where Christ Himself is the cornerstone. Practical outworking of this reality appears when churches engage in collective prayer for guidance, share resources to meet needs, and protect the vulnerable among them. The corporate temple is also a place of accountability; God's presence demands moral purity and compassionate care. When the Spirit convicts corporate sin, confession and repentance restore the temple's sanctity. This communal indwelling segues naturally into recognizing the marks that distinguish a true church.

Having surveyed the church's identity as God's elect priesthood, a diverse body, and a Spirit-built temple, we now turn to the marks that distinguish authentic expressions of this new-covenant community.

8.2 Recognisable Marks of a True Church

8.2.1 Word faithfully preached—gospel at the center

A distinguishing mark of a genuine church is the faithful proclamation of the Word, proclaiming Christ crucified and risen for sinners' justification. This proclamation involves exposition of Scripture in its historical and theological context, ensuring that the gospel is neither diluted nor distorted by cultural fads. The preaching office carries the responsibility of accurately handling the Word of truth, dividing law and gospel so that listeners understand both their sin and their Savior. Faithful preaching addresses head and heart—teaching sound doctrine while igniting worship and obedience. It affirms the full counsel of God: creation, fall, redemption, sanctification, and consummation. When the Word is central, church life orients around hearing, applying, and living out biblical truth. Preaching that honors the text fosters doctrinal unity and guards against error. It also equips the congregation for service, mission, and discipleship. A church that preaches Christ continually reflects the apostolic pattern and invites the Spirit's transformative work.

8.2.2 Sacraments rightly administered—baptism and the Table

The sacraments of baptism and the Lord's Supper materialize the gospel's realities, linking visible signs with invisible grace. Baptism publicly seals the believer's union with Christ in His death and resurrection, initiating entry into the covenant community. Proper administration involves Trinitarian invocation, appropriate candidates, and the mode that coheres with biblical symbolism and communal understanding. The Lord's Supper regularly renews covenant remembrance, calling participants to examine themselves, proclaim the Lord's death, and anticipate His return. Right administration emphasizes both remembrance and participation in Christ's sacrifice, avoiding empty ritualism on one hand and exotic mystery on the other. The sacraments also bind the community together: all who partake affirm shared faith and mutual responsibility. Pastors and elders shepherd these ordinances, ensuring reverence, order, and accessibility. Through faithful sacraments, the church experiences its unity with Christ and with one another.

8.2.3 Loving discipline and pursuit of holiness

A true church cultivates holiness through loving discipline, refusing to permit persistent sin that undermines both individual faith and collective witness. This discipline follows a biblical process: private admonition, small group intervention, and broader communal action if necessary. The goal is restorative rather than punitive—drawing wayward members back into fellowship through repentance and reconciliation. The church's pursuit of holiness extends beyond correcting overt transgressions to nurturing spiritual growth: teaching on moral purity, cultivating inner character, and modeling transparent confession. Corporate worship, mutual accountability, and structured discipleship pathways reinforce holiness as the church's heartbeat. Discipline and pursuit of sanctity demonstrate that grace does not condone sin but empowers transformation. They also reassure seekers that the church takes holiness seriously. By upholding these marks—Word, sacraments, and discipline—the church embodies the corporate dimensions of salvation.

With these distinguishing marks in mind, we next explore how baptism functions as the gateway into the covenant community.

8.3 Baptism: Entrance into the Covenant Community

8.3.1 Union imagery—death, burial, resurrection with Christ

Baptism vividly enacts the believer's union with Christ in His death, burial, and resurrection, symbolizing the believer's old self crucified with Him and new life raised in Him. Immersion signifies burial, emerging from water signifies resurrection. These images reinforce that salvation involves dying to sin and living to God, a reality experienced once but symbolically rehearsed in baptism. As participants are immersed, they identify with Christ's atoning death; as they rise, they claim His victory over death. This union imagery teaches that sanctification flows from this foundational solidarity. Churches teach baptismal candidates the spiritual realities behind the water, linking the ordinance to daily mortification and vivification. Family members and the congregation witness and commit to nurturing the baptized person's new life. Over time, baptism becomes a sacramental milestone that believers recall to recommit their lives to Christ's lordship.

8.3.2 Candidates, mode, and Trinitarian formula—key debates & unity points

Historic debates over candidates (infant vs. believer), mode (immersion vs. sprinkling), and formula (Matthew's tri-part invocation) reflect diverse convictions about covenant membership and symbolism. Believer's baptism emphasizes personal repentance and faith preceding the ordinance, while paedo-baptism underscores covenant inclusion based on familial and covenantal continuity. Mode debates hinge on which best captures biblical symbolism and early-church practice. Yet all traditions agree on the Trinitarian invocation— baptizing in the name of the Father, Son, and Holy Spirit—as the basis for baptism's sacramental validity. These unity points allow diverse churches to recognize one another's baptisms, fostering ecumenical fellowship. Pastors explain the theological rationale behind their chosen practice while acknowledging other faithful expressions. This balance between conviction and charity honors both biblical mandate and historical witness.

8.3.3 Baptismal vows, public witness, and local-church membership

Baptismal vows articulate commitments to Christ and covenant community: renouncing sin, affirming faith in Jesus, and promising obedience to His Word. These vows transform the ceremony from a symbol into a covenantal pact publicly witnessed by the gathered family of faith. Local-church membership often follows baptism, integrating the baptized into a specific congregation's life, responsibilities, and privileges. Membership commits both the individual to the church's care and the church to the individual's discipleship. It provides structures for accountability, service, and fellowship. Churches clarify membership expectations—attendance, support, participation in sacraments, submission to discipline—to ensure clarity and mutual care. This covenantal framework embodies the communal dimensions of salvation institutionalized through baptism.

Having seen how baptism inaugurates entry into the covenant community, we now turn to the Lord's Supper as the ongoing meal of participation in Christ.

8.4 The Lord's Supper: Ongoing Participation in Christ

8.4.1 Covenant renewal meal—remembrance, presence, anticipation

The Lord's Supper functions as a covenant renewal meal in which believers remember Christ's sacrifice, enjoy His spiritual presence, and anticipate His return. Taking the bread and cup re-enacts the Last Supper's covenant-ratifying language—"This is my body... my blood of the covenant"—linking participants to the new covenant promised by Jeremiah. This meal simultaneously commemorates what Christ has done, embeds believers in His ongoing presence through the Spirit, and points forward to the eschatological banquet. Each element serves dual purposes: remembrance of atonement and reception of grace, embodying both retrospective and prospective dimensions of salvation. Regular celebration fosters communal identity and mutual dependence. Preparation involves self-examination, confession, and reconciliation to avoid unworthy participation. As the congregation eats and drinks together, they proclaim the Lord's death until He comes, affirming both unity and mission. Pastors guide both theological reflection and devotional response, ensuring the Supper remains a living, formative practice.

8.4.2 Models of Christ's presence—memorial, spiritual, sacramental, eschatological

Various theological models explain Christ's presence in the Supper: memorial (Zwingli), spiritual-real presence (Calvin), sacramental union (Luther), and eschatological anticipation (many traditions). The memorial view emphasizes the ordinance as a reminder, while spiritual-real presence holds that believers truly partake of Christ's body and blood by the Spirit's virtue. Sacramental union asserts a mysterious joining of bread and body, while eschatological models highlight the Supper's forward-looking dimension as the foretaste of the heavenly banquet. Despite differences, all affirm that the meal is more than a mere symbol—God's presence is uniquely near in this context. Churches educate members on their own tradition's view while encouraging charity toward other perspectives. This rich tapestry of thought deepens appreciation for the Supper's multifaceted significance.

8.4.3 Communion ethics—self-examination, unity, and proclamation of the gospel

Ethical preparation for communion involves self-examination—recognizing sin, seeking forgiveness, and reconciling with others—to ensure both personal integrity and communal harmony. Paul warns that unworthy participation brings judgment, thus prompting each believer to "examine themselves." This self-examination intersects with community; unity is maintained when members forgive grievances and practice "one-another" commands before gathering. Communion also serves as a public proclamation of the gospel: eating together declares belief in Christ's atoning work and communicates that participants belong to Christ's body. Churches incorporate prayer, Scripture reading, and reflections on the gospel's implications, reinforcing both personal repentance and missional commitment. The Supper thus becomes both a place of grace and a training ground for ethical maturity.

With the sacraments of baptism and the Lord's Supper defined as the key ordinances sustaining community, we now turn to the broader fellowship structures that foster koinonia and mutual ministry.

8.5 Koinonia: Fellowship & Mutual Ministry

8.5.1 Acts 2 pattern—shared teaching, meals, prayer, resources

The early church in Jerusalem exemplified koinonia through devotion to apostolic teaching, communal meals, and shared resources (Acts 2:42–47). This pattern demonstrates how spiritual and material fellowship intertwine: listening to the apostles' doctrine shaped belief, breaking bread fostered relational intimacy, and pooled possessions met needs. As a result, the church experienced favor with both God and people, and the Lord added to their number daily. Modern churches reproduce this synergy through small groups that study Scripture, share meals in homes, and coordinate benevolence to support the impoverished. Prayer circles reinforce spiritual solidarity, enabling members to carry one another's burdens. Resource sharing extends to child care, transportation, and crisis relief, transforming individual generosity into communal care. This holistic fellowship model weaves together spiritual formation and social compassion, embodying the gospel's both/and ethos.

8.5.2 "One-another" practices—encouragement, service, forgiveness

Scripture's "one-another" commands—encourage one another, serve one another, forgive one another—provide concrete instructions for cultivating koinonia (Rom 12:10; Jas 5:16). Encouragement involves speaking life into fellow believers, reminding them of God's promises and their own gifts. Service expresses love in tangible ways—providing meals, assisting with jobs, or mentoring through challenges. Forgiveness, often the most difficult, releases offenders from guilt and preserves unity, modeling the Father's pardon of our own sins. These practices require vulnerability and intentionality, as genuine encouragement cannot be faked, service demands sacrifice, and forgiveness often counters natural inclinations. Churches codify these behaviors through ministry teams, mentoring programs, and conflict-resolution training. When one-another practices flourish, congregations reflect the relational texture of the Trinity itself.

8.5.3 Practical structures—small groups, diaconal care, benevolence funds

To sustain koinonia at scale, churches develop practical structures: small groups for deeper relationship, diaconal ministries for organized mercy, and benevolence funds for systematic aid. Small groups of 6–12 people provide safe contexts for confession, accountability, and mutual encouragement. Diaconal care teams train volunteers to identify and assist vulnerable members, coordinating medical visits, meals, and financial support. Benevolence funds, administered transparently, enable prompt response to needs, ensuring no one falls through cracks. Leadership equips these structures with resources, training, and vision, embedding koinonia into church culture. Seasonal emphases—back-to-school drives, holiday meal ministries—activate communal generosity. Over time, these structures become self-sustaining, as newer members caught up in fellowship join in service. This practical outworking of koinonia bridges the gap between theological affirmation and everyday expression of salvation's communal dimensions.

Having explored the foundational fellowship structures of koinonia, our next focus is on how the church maintains holiness and restores unity through loving discipline.

8.6 Church Discipline and Redemptive Restoration

8.6.1 Purity for witness—why discipline matters

The risen Christ calls His church to be a light set on a hill, and that radiance is dimmed whenever unrepentant sin is allowed to fester in the fellowship (Matt 5:14–16). Church discipline therefore protects the credibility of the gospel by preserving a corporate holiness that mirrors God's character (1 Pet 1:15–16). When outsiders see a congregation address sin humbly yet firmly, they witness an ethical seriousness that contrasts with society's moral drift. Discipline also safeguards the weak; unchecked exploitation or immorality corrodes trust and harms vulnerable members (1 Cor 5:6). Moreover, Scripture links corporate purity to spiritual power: the Spirit is grieved where habitual sin is tolerated, stifling worship and witness (Eph 4:30). Congregations that neglect discipline may retain crowds but forfeit transformational presence. Discipline, rightly understood, is an extension of Christ's shepherding love, for He purifies a people zealous for good works (Tit 2:14). It confronts sin not to shame but to heal, exposing the malignant before it metastasizes. A purified church becomes plausibility proof of salvation's communal dimension—demonstrating that grace not only forgives but reforms. Thus discipline belongs to the Great Commission itself, teaching believers to obey all Jesus commanded (Matt 28:20). Awareness of this purpose prepares hearts for the pastoral process that follows.

8.6.2 Pastoral process—private reproof to public action

Jesus sketches a gracious sequence for discipline that begins privately and escalates only as needed (Matt 18:15–17). Step one is personal reproof: a loving conversation aimed at restoring a brother or sister without public exposure. If repentance occurs, the process ends in quiet reconciliation, modeling mercy and confidentiality. Should private appeal fail, two or three witnesses join, both to verify facts and to increase persuasive weight (Deut 19:15). Persistent resistance necessitates telling it to the church—usually through elders—so the covenant family can plead collectively for repentance. Only after repeated refusal does the church remove table fellowship, symbolizing that the person's behavior contradicts their baptismal confession (1 Cor 5:11–13). Throughout, leaders bathe each step in prayer, humility, and transparency, guarding against harshness or gossip. Timelines remain flexible; some issues resolve quickly, others require months of pastoral pursuit. Documentation ensures due process and protects all parties. Discipline always includes an open door for return—if the individual repents, the church joyfully receives them, embodying the Father who runs to embrace prodigals. Understanding this redemptive pathway highlights the ultimate goals at stake.

8.6.3 Goals: repentance, reconciliation, protection of the flock

The primary aim of discipline is repentance—a changed mind that leads to restored relationship with God and neighbor (2 Cor 7:9–10). When a fallen believer turns, heaven rejoices and the church displays the triumph of grace over sin. Reconciliation quickly follows, knitting estranged parties back into affectionate fellowship that seals the community's unity (Col 3:13–15). A secondary goal is deterrence: public resolution warns others of sin's gravity, urging holy fear (1 Tim 5:20). Discipline also shields the flock, preventing leaven from spreading and safeguarding tender consciences (1 Cor 5:6–8). In this way the church acts as a protective enclosure, much like ancient walls that kept predators at bay. Finally, discipline vindicates Christ's name before the watching world, proving that His followers prize holiness as highly as He does. With these objectives in view, discipline becomes an act of courageous love rather than punitive legalism. This same love undergirds the church's leadership structures, the subject of the next section.

8.7 Leadership Offices and Spiritual Authority

8.7.1   Elders/overseers—qualifications   and   shepherding functions

Biblical elders are not corporate executives but under-shepherds who model Christ's humility and guard doctrine (1 Pet 5:1–4). Their qualifications emphasize character—above reproach, hospitable, self-controlled—over charisma (1 Tim 3:2–7). Elders oversee teaching, ensuring the pulpit anchors the church in gospel truth and wards off error (Tit 1:9). They shepherd the flock through visitation, counseling, and prayer, embodying Jesus' tender vigilance. Decision-making among elders operates collegially, reflecting shared responsibility and mutual submission. Regular self-evaluation—asking whether their leadership nurtures holiness—keeps the office from drifting into mere administration. Elders also mentor emerging leaders, multiplying shepherds for future generations. By guarding both doctrine and life, they create an environment where every member can flourish in faith and service.

8.7.2 Deacons—servant-leadership and mercy ministries

Deacons trace their roots to Acts 6, where Spirit-filled servants coordinated food distribution to widows, ensuring equitable care. Their qualifications mirror elders in character but focus less on teaching and more on reliability and compassion (1 Tim 3:8–13). Today, deacons mobilize practical ministries—benevolence, facility stewardship, crisis response—freeing elders for prayer and Word. They serve as conduits of mercy, channeling congregational generosity into tangible relief. Deacons embody servant leadership, inspiring members to value unseen tasks that uphold communal life. Their collaboration with elders exemplifies complementary

141

authority, illustrating that spiritual oversight and practical service are two sides of one pastoral coin.

8.7.3 Congregational participation—the priesthood of all believers and consensus discernment

While elders and deacons hold recognized offices, every believer shares in the priesthood of all saints, contributing spiritual gifts for mutual edification (1 Cor 14:26). Congregational participation includes affirming leaders, discerning major decisions, and exercising disciplined love toward one another. Healthy churches foster open forums where members voice insights, ask questions, and pray corporately about vision. Consensus does not mean unanimity in every detail but broad alignment driven by shared submission to Scripture and Spirit. This participatory ethos guards against authoritarian drift and reinforces communal ownership of mission. Training in biblical discernment equips members to weigh prophetic words, financial proposals, or doctrinal statements. Thus leadership becomes a partnership: offices provide direction; the body provides confirmation, energy, and accountability. From this synergy emerges robust worship, which we explore next.

8.8 Corporate Worship and Formational Liturgy

8.8.1 Rhythm of Word, prayer, song, and sacrament

Historic Christian worship follows a four-fold rhythm: God speaks, His people respond, they commune at the Table, and He commissions them back into the world. The liturgy opens with a call to worship—Scripture announcing God's initiative—followed by songs and prayers of adoration. Confession and assurance root hearts in grace, preparing minds for the preached Word. Sermons expound Scripture's redemptive storyline and apply it to contemporary life, shaping worldview. The Lord's Supper then embodies the message, enabling participants to taste and see the gospel. Closing songs and benedictions send the congregation as witnesses. This rhythm forms spiritual muscle memory: week after week, believers rehearse God's actions and their response, aligning affections and habits to the kingdom.

8.8.2 Church calendar and ordinances shaping spiritual imagination

Beyond weekly gatherings, the church calendar—Advent, Lent, Easter, Pentecost—narrates the life of Christ across the year. These seasons immerse congregations in gospel milestones: anticipation, incarnation, atonement, resurrection, and mission. Observing these cycles counters cultural calendars dominated by consumer holidays, re-centering imagination on redemption history. Ordinances like baptism and communion punctuate the calendar, offering tactile anchors for memory and hope. They teach children and new believers by embodied experience rather than lecture alone. The calendar also paces discipleship, inviting fasting, celebration, lament, and joy at appropriate intervals.

8.8.3 Contextualizing worship—unity amid cultural diversity

Global Christianity encompasses myriad musical styles, art forms, and languages, all capable of conveying orthodox worship. Contextualization affirms local culture while submitting content to biblical boundaries. African rhythms, Latin American dance, Asian tonalities, and Western hymns each express facets of divine glory. Translation of liturgy into heart languages honors Pentecost's reversal of Babel (Acts 2). Yet diversity seeks unity: core components—Trinitarian focus, Scripture reading, gospel proclamation, and sacraments—remain non-negotiable. Mutual learning across cultures enriches all; Western churches recover lament from the Global South, while majority-world congregations glean systematic depth from Reformation traditions. Such exchange displays the multifaceted wisdom of God. Shaped by cross-cultural worship, congregations are primed for mission, our next theme.

8.9 Mission as Communal Vocation

8.9.1 Sentness—church as embassy of the kingdom

Jesus breathes His Spirit on the disciples and says, "As the Father has sent me, so I send you" (John 20:21). Local congregations function as embassies of heaven, showcasing kingdom culture in foreign territory. This sent identity shapes everything—from preaching to budgeting—aligning priorities with reaching the lost. Members recognize that Sunday gatherings constitute mission headquarters, not the terminus of faith. Churches map neighborhoods, pray over workplaces, and equip members to engage in civic life as salt and light. Joint evangelism projects—alpha courses, sports outreaches—harness collective gifts for local impact.

8.9.2 Mercy and justice initiatives—embodying good news

Gospel proclamation gains credibility when coupled with acts of mercy and justice. Early Christians cared for plague victims, turning cities toward Christ; modern churches tutor children, combat human trafficking, and advocate for refugees. Such initiatives arise from theological conviction: the kingdom heralds justice rolled down like mighty waters (Amos 5:24). Mercy projects flow from the Table, where bread for souls overflows into bread for stomachs. Churches form partnerships with NGOs, offering volunteers and spiritual support. Serving together bonds members, disciples youth, and confronts systemic evil.

8.9.3 Global partnerships and church-planting movements

Mission extends to the ends of the earth, compelling churches to send and support workers among unreached peoples (Rom 15:20–24). Healthy partnerships involve reciprocal learning: Western finances empower indigenous leadership, while majority-world perspectives challenge Western blind spots. Short-term trips morph into long-term church-planting teams, multiplying congregations that reproduce worship, fellowship, and sacraments in contextual forms. Prayer networks intercede for breakthrough; digital platforms allow real-time encouragement. Mission agencies collaborate with local churches, ensuring theological depth and holistic strategy. The cycle of gathering and scattering thus continues until Christ returns.

As congregations labor locally and globally, their sacramental life fuels hope for the ultimate gathering—now we consider how Table and font shape eschatological longing.

8.10 Sacramental Hope: From Table to Feast

8.10.1 Lord's Supper as foretaste of the marriage supper

Every communion service is an hors d'oeuvre of the coming marriage supper of the Lamb (Rev 19:7–9). The small piece of bread and sip of wine whisper of a banquet where hunger and sorrow are banished. By eating together in anticipation, believers rehearse future fellowship, nurturing perseverance amid present affliction. This forward gaze infuses the meal with joy: even in persecution, saints taste victory. Pastors remind congregations that each "Amen" at the Table echoes toward the day when faith will become sight.

8.10.2 Baptism anticipating bodily resurrection

Just as baptism symbolizes burial and resurrection, it also previews the bodily renewal believers will experience at Christ's return (Rom 8:11). The descent beneath water foreshadows physical death's brief reign; the ascent proclaims its defeat. This eschatological promise comforts the sick and aging, affirming that their hope is not disembodied bliss but embodied glory. Baptismal anniversaries provide occasions to revisit this promise, strengthening resolve to live as resurrection people in a decaying world.

8.10.3 Escatological community—new Jerusalem as perfected fellowship

Revelation envisions a city where God dwells with His people, wiping away every tear and erasing every fracture (Rev 21:1–4). Sacramental life—corporate meals, covenant water—prepares the church for that perfected fellowship. Each act of reconciliation, each shared cup, pre-figures the harmony of the new Jerusalem. The church's multicultural worship anticipates the nations bringing their glory into the city's light. Hope of this destiny fuels faithfulness in community life today, for believers labor knowing their communal bonds will continue into eternity.

Conclusion

The journey of being saved unfolds most fully within the context of a faithful community, where sacraments seal our identity in Christ and shared life refines individual faith. Through baptism we enter the covenant family, and at the Table we continually proclaim Christ's death until He returns. In fellowship and discipline, leadership and worship, the church becomes both laboratory and embassy of the new creation, demonstrating the gospel's power to reconcile, heal, and renew. As the community lives out these rhythms together, it anticipates the great eschatological feast when every redeemed heart will gather in perfected unity around the Lamb, forever celebrating the depth and breadth of God's saving grace.

Chapter 9. Perseverance: Kept by God, Active in Faith

Every genuine disciple soon discovers that the Christian race is a marathon, not a sprint, and that finishing well requires more than human stamina. Scripture insists that the saints cross the finish line only because an unfailing God holds them fast, even as they press on with Spirit-empowered diligence (John 10:28; Phil 3:12–14). This mysterious partnership—divine preservation and active perseverance—forms the backbone of Christian hope: the Father decrees our security, the Son intercedes for our safety, and the Spirit fuels our persistence. Yet that assurance never breeds passivity; instead, it summons vigilance, prayer, and obedience, forging character in the crucible of trials and temptations. In this chapter we explore how sovereign grace and responsive faith intertwine across ordinary disciplines, communal exhortation, and eschatological vision, equipping believers to endure every season until they stand blameless before the throne.

9.1 Two Hands of Perseverance: Divine Preservation & Human Persistence

9.1.1 "No one can snatch them" — security in the Father's grip

Jesus frames the believer's security in familial terms, likening the Father's hold to an unbreakable clasp that encircles every sheep (John 10:27-29). The imagery evokes both tenderness and power: a shepherd who calls each lamb by name yet possesses the strength to fend off every threat. Divine preservation is therefore not a static guarantee hanging over an indifferent saint; it is the living embrace of a Father who never slumbers, whose omnipotence and covenant love converge to protect His children. Election before time, justification at conversion, and the ongoing intercession of the resurrected Son all serve this single purpose — that none given to Christ will be lost (John 6:39). Even when believers stumble, the Shepherd's staff hooks them back, preventing total ruin. Satan's accusations fall powerless because the Father's verdict of righteousness stands sealed by the Spirit. This assurance does not depend on fluctuating moods or moral perfection but on God's immutable nature: He cannot deny Himself (2 Tim 2:13). As storms of persecution or seasons of darkness descend, saints recall that beneath every trembling grip of faith lies the Almighty's unfailing grasp. From this fortress of divine security flows courage to fight sin, endure hardship, and advance the gospel without fear of ultimate defeat. Such courage, however, never drifts into passivity; it ignites responsible action, which the next subsection explores.

9.1.2 "Work out your salvation" — believer's active endurance

Paul's summons to "work out your own salvation with fear and trembling" (Phil 2:12) underscores that secure sheep are also striving runners. This work is not a quest to earn favor already bestowed; it is the strenuous application of grace to every sphere of life. Active endurance involves daily choices — turning from temptation, confessing sin promptly, pursuing good works, and guarding doctrine. The Spirit energizes these efforts from within, yet believers must still wield spiritual disciplines like a soldier polishing his armor. Scripture memorization arms the mind; fasting sharpens dependence; intentional rest prevents burnout. Active perseverance also demands a long obedience in one direction, resisting the modern impulse for quick fixes and instant gratification. Faithfulness in small, unseen duties — kind words to a spouse, honest taxes, hidden prayers — weaves a tapestry of resilience. When setbacks occur, persevering saints rise again, applying gospel remedies rather than wallowing in shame. Far from negating security, this vigor validates it, for only hearts gripped by God exert sustained, joyful effort. The partner verse in Philippians clarifies the synergy: God works in us "both to will and to work," even as we labor (Phil 2:13). Recognizing both realities prepares us to appreciate their mysterious interplay, which the next subsection clarifies.

9.1.3 Union without passivity — synergy, not symmetry

Perseverance thrives in the soil of union with Christ, where branches draw life from the Vine yet still bear fruit by abiding (John 15:4-5). This union is never a 50-50 contract; God supplies 100 percent of enabling grace while believers respond with 100 percent of dependent effort. The relationship is synergistic (working together) but not symmetric (equal contribution). Such nuance guards against twin errors: legalistic self-reliance and fatalistic complacency. The believer's activity is derivative, like the moon reflecting the sun—real light, but borrowed brilliance. From union flows motivation, not mere obligation; we strive because His life pulses within us. Conversely, union prevents pride when progress occurs, reminding us that "apart from Him we can do nothing." Pastors help congregations keep synergy in view by pairing imperatives with indicatives: "Forgive one another" (imperative) because "God in Christ forgave you" (indicative). Counseling applies the same framework: confront sin firmly yet ground repentance in gospel identity. When saints grasp this integration, perseverance becomes a relationship rather than a solo project. With the theological framework set—the Father's grip, the believer's grit, the union's synergy—we now investigate how assurance and perseverance relate in lived experience.

9.2 Assurance and Perseverance: Distinguishing but Relating

9.2.1 Assurance as confidence; perseverance as continuation

Assurance answers the question, "Am I truly in Christ now?" while perseverance addresses, "Will I still be in Christ at the end?" Both derive from the same covenant grace but occupy different experiential horizons. Assurance is a settled confidence birthed by the Spirit's witness that we are God's children (Rom 8:16). Perseverance is that same Spirit-led life stretched across time, continuing in faith and obedience until death or Christ's return. The distinction prevents confusion: a believer may enjoy present assurance yet still heed calls to vigilance. Conversely, temporary lack of assurance does not equal loss of salvation, for perseverance often survives on mustard-seed faith. The Bible keeps these concepts in tandem, offering promises for assurance (Rom 8:38-39) and warnings to fuel perseverance (Heb 3:12-14). Healthy churches teach both, avoiding extremes of presumption or crippling doubt. Such teaching liberates believers to rest in Christ's sufficiency while striving toward maturity. This rest-while-running paradox shapes responses to seasons of doubt, our next focus.

9.2.2 Seasons of doubt within unbroken faith

Even giants of faith—Asaph, Job, John the Baptist—walked through valleys where assurance dimmed (Ps 73:2-3; Matt 11:3). Doubt often arises from intense suffering, lingering sin struggles, or intellectual questions. During such seasons, perseverance operates like subterranean roots sustaining a leafless tree. The Spirit keeps faith alive beneath emotional frost, assuring believers by Word and sacrament even when feelings fade. Spiritual friendships provide external reminders of gospel truth, echoing God's faithfulness when inner voices falter. Over time, doubts can refine faith, stripping it of naïve assumptions and deepening reliance on Christ's objective work. Pastoral counsel directs doubters to meditate on God's character, recount past deliverances, and maintain corporate worship attendance. Gradually assurance rekindles, emerging sturdier than before. These experiences teach believers not to trust the barometer of mood but the lighthouse of Scripture. Recognizing doubt's temporary nature leads us to evaluate the signs that usually reinforce certainty, explored in the next subsection.

9.2.3 Signs of life that reinforce certainty

Just as a doctor checks pulse, breathing, and reflex response to confirm life, Scripture offers vital signs for spiritual vitality. Ongoing repentance—sorrow over sin and turning toward righteousness—indicates living faith. Growing love for God and neighbor, hunger for Scripture, persistence in prayer, and willingness to forgive reveal the Spirit's fruit (Gal 5:22-23). Endurance under trial, though painful, testifies to genuine rootage (Jas 1:12). These signs are not boxes to earn favor but evidences that grace is operative. Regular self-examination, guided by 2 Corinthians 13:5, helps believers discern such fruit without sliding into morbid introspection. Communal affirmation also matters—mature saints point out growth unseen by the one who experiences it. Observing these indicators revives assurance and fuels fresh perseverance. With assurance clarified, we now explore ordinary means God uses to sustain extraordinary endurance.

9.3 Ordinary Means That Sustain Extraordinary Endurance

9.3.1 Word-anchored hope: daily Scripture as ballast

Scripture functions like ballast in a ship's hull, stabilizing the vessel against crosswinds of suffering and false teaching. Daily intake—reading, meditation, memorization—cements promises in the heart, providing ready ammunition when discouragement or temptation strikes. Stories of Joseph's resilience, David's repentance, and Paul's perseverance expand the imagination of hope. Doctrinal passages frame suffering within God's redemptive plan, preventing interpretive chaos. The Spirit personalizes texts at providential moments; a psalm read at dawn becomes the anchor for an unexpected crisis by noon. Long-term exposure forms mental grooves of truth, displacing lies that fuel despair. Small-group Bible studies reinforce individual reading, offering interpretation checks and mutual encouragement. Over years, a Scripture-saturated mind instinctively filters experience through gospel lenses, a crucial mechanism for perseverance.

9.3.2 Prayer-infused tenacity: asking, seeking, knocking

Persistent prayer resembles marathon breathing—rhythmic inhalation of grace and exhalation of need. Jesus' parable of the importunate widow (Luke 18:1-8) portrays perseverance in prayer as both privilege and command. Through repeated petition, believers cultivate dependence, humility, and attentiveness to God's timing. Lament prayers vent sorrow honestly, preventing bitterness; thanksgiving prayers rehearse past mercies, strengthening faith. Intercessory prayer knits hearts together—praying saints persevere not only for themselves but for the entire body. Corporate prayer meetings become spiritual furnaces where coals of individual devotion ignite collective zeal. Answered prayers, whether dramatic or subtle, build a memory bank of divine faithfulness, fortifying resolve for future trials.

9.3.3 Sacramental nourishment: Table and fellowship fortifying resolve

The Lord's Table offers tangible grace, nourishing perseverance through taste, touch, and communal unity (1 Cor 10:16-17). The bread and cup preach that Christ's finished work continues to sustain stumbling saints, inviting them to feed on grace afresh. Regular participation reminds believers that perseverance is not self-sourced; it flows from ongoing communion with Christ. Fellowship around the Table also reaffirms corporate bonds, ensuring no one runs alone. Post-communion conversations often lead to practical care—rides for medical appointments, financial help, or intercessory partnerships—that bolster endurance. Baptism anniversaries likewise spark reflection on God's keeping power since the waters, prompting recommitment. These ordinary means— Word, prayer, sacrament—constitute spiritual diet and exercise, enabling long-haul faithfulness. Yet God often accelerates growth through furnace seasons, our next section.

9.4 Perseverance in the Furnace: Trials, Suffering, and Discipline

9.4.1 Refining fire producing steadfastness

James exhorts believers to count trials as joy because they refine faith much like heat purifies gold (Jas 1:2-4). The metaphor underscores that impurities surface only under high temperatures; likewise, hidden idols and fears emerge when pressure mounts. As endurance completes its work, believers mature, lacking nothing in spiritual resilience. Physiologically, muscles strengthen by resistance; spiritually, steadfastness grows under adversity. Trial-forged believers develop empathetic capacity, comforting others with comfort received. They also gain testimonial authority—words carry weight when forged in personal crucible. Diaries and prayer journals kept during trials become future monuments of grace, reminding saints of God's past interventions. When the furnace cools, refined character remains, ready for next assignments.

9.4.2 Fatherly discipline preventing shipwreck

Hebrews portrays suffering not merely as impersonal hardship but as fatherly discipline shaping holiness (Heb 12:5-11). Discipline differs from punitive wrath; it trains children for righteousness and yields peaceful fruit. Recognizing this paternal motive reframes affliction from divine abandonment to divine investment. Such insight curbs self-pity and fosters submission: "Not my will but Yours." Discipline custom-fit to individual vulnerabilities deters spiritual shipwreck by exposing and correcting course early. Congregational teaching on discipline helps believers interpret hardships, avoiding satanic lies that God is indifferent. Pastoral care accompanies sufferers, translating theology into comfort.

9.4.3 Sharing Christ's sufferings — vocational cross-bearing

Peter admonishes saints not to be surprised by fiery ordeals but to rejoice in sharing Christ's sufferings (1 Pet 4:12-13). This participatory lens transforms persecution and vocational sacrifices into fellowship with Jesus. Missionaries leaving home, professionals refusing unethical promotions, parents caring for special-needs children—all bear crosses uniquely tailored to their calling. Such cross-bearing enlarges capacity for glory, for "if we suffer with Him, we shall also reign with Him" (2 Tim 2:12). The Spirit turns pain into a platform for witness—colleagues observe peace amid pressure, families see forgiveness under injustice. Over time, shared suffering bonds believers into a resilient community, echoing early-church solidarity. This furnace-fashioned fellowship returns us to corporate vigilance, the subject of the next section.

9.5 Apostasy Warnings & Genuine Faith: Reading Hebrews & Others

9.5.1 Exhortations as God's means to keep saints alert

Hebrews bristles with "if" clauses that jolt complacent hearts, yet these solemn warnings are not threats of inevitable doom but instruments in God's preserving hand (Heb 3:12-14). Each exhortation functions like a guardrail along a mountain road, preventing the pilgrim from sleep-walking off the cliff of unbelief. By addressing the entire congregation—"Take care, brothers"—the writer enlists every member in mutual vigilance, transforming perseverance into a shared project rather than a solo quest. The warnings expose the deceitfulness of sin, a slow hardening that often masquerades as harmless compromise until the conscience calcifies. They remind readers that drifting usually begins with neglect—skipped gatherings, unmortified grumbling—long before outright rebellion appears. Far from undermining assurance, the warnings underline its dynamic nature: confidence is maintained by heeding God's voice "today," not by resting on yesterday's profession. Pastors apply these texts by urging continual self-examination, not to foster morbid doubt but to keep faith responsive and supple. When believers feel the sting of a warning, they are driven back to the throne of grace for fresh mercy, illustrating how God uses admonition to draw His children closer. The Spirit wields these passages like a skilled surgeon, cutting only to heal, exposing cancerous complacency so that repentance may flow. Churches that preach the whole counsel of God—promises and perils—cultivate soberminded disciples who neither presume on grace nor shrink from it. The apostolic pattern therefore marries security with seriousness, ensuring the flock remains wide-awake until the Chief Shepherd appears. Understanding warnings as means, not contradictions, prepares us to distinguish temporary enthusiasm from rooted trust, explored next.

9.5.2 Temporary belief vs. rooted trust — parable of soils

Jesus' parable of the sower reveals that not every positive response to the gospel ripens into enduring fruit (Luke 8:13-15). Rocky-soil hearers receive the word with joy, yet their superficial root system withers when persecution or testing comes. Thorny-soil hearers believe for a season, but the cares of life, riches, and pleasures choke emerging shoots before harvest. Good-soil believers, by contrast, cling to the word with noble and patient hearts, yielding fruit through endurance. The parable teaches that genuine faith is identified not by initial exuberance but by sustained obedience amid adversity. Spiritual emotions are not unimportant—joy is fitting—but they are inadequate without rooted conviction. Trials act as spiritual audits, revealing which hearts are deeply anchored and which merely accessorized with religion. Pastoral follow-up of new converts is thus crucial: teaching, fellowship, and accountability help tender plants send roots into Christ before scorching heat arrives. Likewise, discipleship must address worldly anxieties and materialism, regularly pruning the thorns that threaten to suffocate devotion. The parable reassures persevering saints: slow, steady fruitfulness pleases God more than flash-in-the-pan fervor. It also cautions churches against equating attendance spikes with revival; true growth is measured by harvest season, not planting day. By embedding endurance into conversion expectations, leaders inoculate believers against disillusionment when hardships arise. This horticultural wisdom sets the stage for biblical case studies that contrast abandonment with perseverance.

9.5.3 Case studies: Demas, Judas, and the perseverance contrast

Scripture's biographies crystallize doctrine in flesh and blood, none more sobering than Judas and Demas. Judas inhabited Jesus' inner circle, witnessed miracles, and performed ministry, yet love of money and satanic collusion drove him to betrayal (John 12:6; 13:27). His tragic end demonstrates that external proximity to Christ is no substitute for transformed allegiance. Demas, once a fellow worker beside Paul, deserted "because he loved this present world," revealing divided affections that finally tipped toward apostasy (2 Tim 4:10). In stark contrast stand Peter and John Mark: both stumbled, yet genuine faith, buoyed by Christ's intercession and communal restoration, prevailed. Their stories illustrate that failure does not equal final falling; repentance reaffirms authenticity. The juxtaposition of Demas and Mark teaches churches to hold discipline and mercy together, discerning trajectories over isolated incidents. Contemporary parallels appear whenever public figures renounce faith: the church grieves, examines root causes, and renews its own vigilance. Personal reflection on these narratives fosters humility—"Let anyone who thinks he stands take heed"—and hope that Christ can reclaim the wavering (1 Cor 10:12). Such case studies ground warnings and promises in lived reality, motivating believers to seek communal safeguards, our next section's focus.

9.6 Communal Vigilance: "Exhort One Another Daily"

9.6.1 Mutual encouragement combating deceitfulness of sin

Hebrews mandates a daily rhythm of mutual exhortation to avert the heart-hardening effect of sin's deceit (Heb 10:24-25). Encouragement here is more than cheerleading; it is gospel-infused reminder of truths prone to leak from memory. Sin deceives by disguising itself as harmless, urgent, or advantageous; a brother's timely word pierces that illusion, restoring clarity. Regular gatherings—Sunday worship, mid-week groups, informal coffees—create contexts for these soul-saving conversations. When believers share testimonies of God's faithfulness, they refresh weary spirits and recalibrate perspectives warped by cultural narratives. Encouragement also involves celebration of progress, affirming fledgling obedience that doubters might overlook in themselves. Such affirmations supply energy for further perseverance, proving that edification is a renewable resource. In digital age isolation, intentional check-ins via text or call serve as lifelines, breaking the spell of loneliness that breeds temptation. Leaders model vulnerability, inviting the congregation into mutual care rather than one-way exhortation. Over time, a culture of encouragement raises the congregation's spiritual temperature, making corporate apostasy exponentially harder. This vigilant warmth naturally leans on collective memory, our next subtheme.

9.6.2 Corporate memory of God's past faithfulness

Psalm after psalm commands one generation to commend God's works to the next (Ps 145:4-7). Corporate memory operates like a spiritual library, storing testimonies of deliverance, provision, and revival to be retrieved during crises. Congregations cultivate this memory through storytelling liturgies—annual "Ebenezer" services, baptism testimonies, and shared journals of answered prayers. Remembering resets anxiety gauges: if God opened the Red Sea, He can part present waters. Historical catechesis links modern believers with saints of old, drawing courage from martyrs and reformers who finished well. Visual symbols—stained glass, memorial plaques, baptismal photos—anchor memory in space, transforming sanctuaries into living museums of grace. When newcomers hear seasoned saints recount cancer healings or war-time protections, they inherit a heritage of trust. Corporate memory thus feeds hope, which fuels perseverance. It also erects warning signposts: recalling Israel's wilderness unbelief cautions against repeating their errors (1 Cor 10:6). Guided by communal remembrance, churches practice restorative discipline, which safeguards long-term holiness.

9.6.3 Restorative discipline safeguarding long-haul holiness

Galatians envisions believers gently restoring anyone caught in sin, watching themselves lest they also be tempted (Gal 6:1-2). This restorative aim distinguishes gospel discipline from punitive expulsion. Accountability groups, elder shepherding visits, and peer confession networks create nets that catch slips before they become slides. When formal discipline is required, the congregation mourns, prays, and pleads for repentance, demonstrating love even in firmness. Joy erupts when a wanderer returns, illustrating discipline's success and reinforcing community bonds. Regular teaching on discipline demystifies the process and pre-emptively disarms defensive reactions. A church seasoned in gentle restoration offers refuge for strugglers, countering culture's cancel reflex. By knitting discipline into communal rhythms of worship and fellowship, perseverance gains a collective backbone. This shared vigilance naturally dovetails with alertness to spiritual predators, our next section's concern.

9.7 Spiritual Warfare & Watchfulness

9.7.1 Alertness against satanic schemes

Peter likens Satan to a prowling lion seeking someone to devour, underscoring the need for sober, watchful resistance (1 Pet 5:8-9). Alertness entails recognizing temptation's timing—often following spiritual highs or prolonged fatigue—and fortifying vulnerable flanks. Saints study enemy playbooks in Scripture: deceptive questioning (Eden), accusatory condemnation (Job), and counterfeit signs (Revelation). Vigilance also involves discerning cultural currents that subtly erode biblical convictions. Intercessory prayer stands guard at city gates, calling on heaven's armies to thwart demonic plots against families, leaders, and new believers. Fasting amplifies discernment, tuning spiritual senses to faint whispers of compromise. When demonic oppression surfaces—whether in addictive bondage or invasive lies—believers employ scriptural rebuke, reminding the adversary of Christ's victory. Standing firm in faith is communal; isolated soldiers are easy prey, but shield-wall formation repels charges. Testimonies of deliverance fortify faith, proving that resistance is not futile. From this alert footing, believers don armor designed for long campaigns.

9.7.2 Armor re-examined for marathon, not sprint

Paul's armor imagery suits a marathon soldier who must march and stand for life, not merely fight one battle (Eph 6:10-18). The belt of truth secures identity against shifting cultural definitions; it must be tightened daily through Word intake. The breastplate of righteousness guards heart affections, reminding saints that positional justification resists shame's flaming darts. Gospel shoes provide traction on rugged terrain, enabling swift movement toward both service and refuge. The shield of faith—not a small buckler but a door-sized barrier—interlocks with others', illustrating collective defense. The helmet of salvation protects thought life, especially against despair in protracted trials. Finally, the sword of the Spirit—the spoken Word—requires practice; memorized verses become ready thrusts when temptation lunges. Prayer saturates the ensemble like oil, preventing joints from seizing up during extended strain. Churches host "armor workshops" where members identify weak points and custom-fit biblical promises. This durable outfitting prepares saints to pray continually the petition Jesus taught.

9.7.3 Praying "Lead us not into temptation" as daily posture

The Lord's Prayer closes with a plea for deliverance, shaping watchfulness into daily liturgy (Matt 6:13). Voicing this line each morning acknowledges frailty and invites God's shepherding through the day's minefield. The petition combines humility—"I am capable of falling"—with faith—"You are able to keep me." It covers both inward lures and external traps, from subtle pride to sudden persecution. Families incorporate the prayer at breakfast; teams recite it before mission trips; individuals whisper it in rush-hour traffic. Over time, the phrase triggers situational alerts: when gossip beckons, the Spirit recalls "deliver us"; when unethical shortcuts appear, "lead us not" surfaces like a warning light. The community that prays thus collectively cultivates a culture of dependency rather than bravado. Having armed minds with this posture, endurance is further propelled by forward-looking reward, our next exploration.

9.8 Eschatological Motivation: Reward, Crown, & "Well Done"

9.8.1 "For the joy set before Him" — Christ as model motivator

Hebrews presents Jesus enduring the cross "for the joy set before Him," revealing that future glory fuels present grit (Heb 12:1-3). Likewise, believers fix eyes on coming joy—a perfected world, face-to-face fellowship, sin's extinction—to sustain momentum. Meditation on promised joy recalibrates pain meters; light momentary afflictions become ladders to eternal weight. Hymns that celebrate resurrection, sermons on the new earth, and artwork depicting the throne room saturate imagination with hope. Joy motivation does not cheapen sacrifice; it dignifies it, framing hardship as seed for everlasting harvest. When persecuted saints sing in prison, they echo their Master's forward gaze. Missionaries risking disease or martyrdom testify that anticipated joy eclipses temporal loss. Church calendars placing Resurrection Sunday at the center preach hope annually, but weekly communion whispers the same promise. By tracing Jesus' pattern, believers discover that anticipation can transform endurance from gritted teeth to eager stride.

9.8.2 Crowns of life, righteousness, glory

New-Testament writers speak of crowns awaiting the faithful: life for steadfast sufferers, righteousness for those loving Christ's appearing, and glory for faithful shepherds (Jas 1:12; 2 Tim 4:8; 1 Pet 5:4). These crowns symbolize divine commendation—public affirmation that persevering faith delighted God. The prospect of reward is not mercenary; it is relational, anticipating the Father's smile and the Master's "Well done." Crowns vary to honor diverse callings, proving God notices hidden labors—nursery duty, quiet intercession, sacrificial giving. Preachers remind congregants that every cup of cold water has eternal echo. Knowing that investments reap imperishable dividends loosens grip on earthly accolades. Saints gladly endure obscurity, financial loss, or cultural scorn, confident that heavenly stock never crashes. The hope of crowns also curbs compromise: why trade everlasting honor for fleeting pleasure? Anticipation of reward thus sharpens ethical resolve and infuses perseverance with purpose.

9.8.3 New-creation vision fueling present grit

Revelation's vision of a renewed cosmos—tears wiped, death defeated, nations healed—casts perseverance against an epic horizon (Rev 21:5-7). Believers picture resurrected bodies brimming with energy, cultural treasures purified and accessible, labor devoid of futility. This eschatological panorama infuses vocational perseverance: scientists tackling disease, artists crafting beauty, activists pursuing justice, all anticipating their work's continuity in the new earth. Hope of cosmic renewal also births ecological stewardship, treating creation as future inheritance rather than disposable stage prop. In suffering, the vision reminds saints that every sigh is scheduled for reversal. Liturgy that concludes with a sending, "Go in peace to love and serve," links weekly worship to cosmic mission. Small groups study prophetic texts not for speculation timelines but for ethical traction—holiness hastens the day. Thus, eschatological hope operates like a spiritual adrenaline shot, propelling marathoners toward the tape.

With hearts aimed at eternal joy and fortified by vigilant warfare, believers adopt practical habits that help them finish well—patterns we now explore in habits of a finishing life.

9.9 Habits of a Finishing Life: Discipline, Resilience, and Renewal

9.9.1 Rule of life — ordered rhythms that prevent drift

A well-crafted rule of life acts like a trellis, supporting the vine of devotion so it grows upward rather than sprawling in disorder. Early Christians adopted such frameworks, gathering for fixed-hour prayers that punctuated labor with worship (Acts 3:1). Modern disciples who schedule Scripture meditation, intercession, hospitality, and exercise discover that intentionality breeds freedom rather than legalism. Crafting a rule begins with prayerful audit: What pursuits nourish faith and which choke it? Once priorities are clear, they are mapped onto weekly and seasonal calendars, allowing for both structure and spontaneity. Goals remain realistic—better fifteen unhurried minutes in the Word than an ambitious plan that collapses by Wednesday. The rule flexes with life stage: new parents shorten silent retreats while emphasizing corporate worship; retirees expand mentoring slots. Accountability partners review rules quarterly, celebrating consistency and adjusting unrealistic aims. Digital boundaries find place in the rule, curbing late-night scrolling that dulls morning prayer. Tithing and generosity schedules guard against lifestyle creep, directing funds to mission early each month rather than with leftovers. Sabbatical planning— whether a day hike or multi-week study leave—anchors long-range sustainability. The rule is not carved in granite; it evolves like a living document as callings shift. Written copies posted on refrigerators or phone lock-screens keep commitments visible when motivation lags. Families craft shared rules, synchronizing meal blessings and service projects to weave perseverance into household culture. Over years, an intentional rule transforms isolated pious acts into a cohesive journey that propels runners toward the prize (1 Cor 9:24-27).

9.9.2 Sabbath, celebration, and strategic rest

Perseverance requires rhythm, not relentless pace; therefore God embedded Sabbath into creation before commandments into stone (Gen 2:2-3). Weekly cessation from vocational striving re-teaches hearts that identity rests in grace, not productivity. Planning for Sabbath involves front-loading tasks, communicating boundaries to colleagues, and trusting unfinished lists to divine providence. Rest includes corporate worship, shared meals, walks, naps, music—activities that restore rather than deplete. Celebration partners with rest, marking milestones—graduations, baptisms, anniversaries—with feasts that echo Israel's festivals (Deut 16:15). Such rejoicing inoculates against grim stoicism, reminding pilgrims that the journey ends in joy. Strategic rest extends beyond weekly cadence to sabbaticals: pastors rotate out for study breaks; professionals schedule silent retreats; caregivers secure respite care. Technology fasts form mini-Sabbaths, quieting digital noise to hear God's whisper. Rest also entails sleep hygiene—dark rooms, consistent bedtimes—honoring bodily limits given by a Creator who "gives to His beloved sleep" (Ps 127:2). Physical recreation—cycling, gardening, dance—releases endorphins that combat emotional fatigue. Couples practice date-Sabbaths, protecting marital intimacy that fuels mutual perseverance. Congregations embed rest into program calendars, resisting event gluttony that saps volunteer stamina. By weaving Sabbath and celebration into lifestyle, believers run with sustainable cadence, avoiding the burnout that sidelines many promising racers.

9.9.3 Seasons of recalibration — retreats, mentoring, legacy planning

Even with daily rules and weekly rests, long races demand periodic course corrections. Spiritual retreats—whether a solitary day at a monastery or a weekend with a small cohort—

create space to examine soul health under the Spirit's searchlight (Ps 139:23-24). Silence during retreats uncovers subterranean motives; journaling captures insights before they evaporate in routine. Mentoring relationships offer external perspective: seasoned saints ask probing questions, share cautionary tales, and impart vocational wisdom shaped by decades of finish-line focus (2 Tim 2:2). Mid-life recalibration may prompt vocation shifts, ministry sabbaticals, or renewed educational pursuits to align gifts with evolving needs. Annual vision days help families or teams revisit mission statements, budget priorities, and spiritual goals, ensuring drift is corrected early. Legacy planning steers resources toward eternal dividends—writing ethical wills, establishing scholarship funds, discipling grandchildren—so the influence of a persevering life multiplies beyond the grave (Prov 13:22). Health check-ups, counseling intensives, and marriage retreats fold into recalibration, addressing physical and relational wear before crises erupt. Churches facilitate group pilgrimages to historic revival sites or justice ministries, expanding horizons and rekindling passion. Sabbatical journals become archives for future generations, chronicling detours, breakthroughs, and God's fidelity. After recalibration, believers re-enter routines with clarified purpose and renewed vigor, poised to persevere with sharper focus.

Intentional habits anchor the long race, but the melody of perseverance resolves in worship, where saints attribute every kept step to the God who preserves—an anthem captured in the closing doxology.

9.10 Doxology of Preservation: Glory to the Faithful God

9.10.1 Jude's benediction as daily doxology

Jude closes his brief epistle not with strategies but with song: "Now to Him who is able to keep you from stumbling..." (Jude 24-25). This benediction encapsulates the whole doctrine of perseverance in a burst of praise, shifting focus from human exertion to divine capability. Reciting the doxology daily recenters labor on the Keeper rather than the kept. Worship teams arrange Jude's words into choruses; parents teach them as bedtime prayers; solo travelers whisper them on jetways. The verse's two verbs—keep and present—span the journey and the destination, assuring saints of protection now and blamelessness then. Glory, majesty, dominion, and authority pile up like mounting waves, drowning fears of failure. In corporate gatherings, reading Jude's doxology after sermons seals exhortations with adoration, turning knowledge into kneeling. Personalizing the pronouns—"to Him who is able to keep me"—deepens intimacy without shrinking grandeur. Such worship fuels obedience: hearts awed by majesty sprint gladly toward holiness.

9.10.2 Testimonies of kept saints—personal and biblical

Stories translate theology into flesh, and testimonies of divine keeping kindle fresh faith. Scripture supplies prototypes: Daniel preserved in lions' den, Elijah sustained under broom tree, and Mary clinging to promise amid scandal (Dan 6:22; 1 Kgs 19:5-8; Luke 1:38-45). Contemporary narratives echo these themes—missionaries spared in coups, recovering addicts celebrating decades of sobriety, elderly widows radiant with hope. Testimony nights in local churches spotlight such accounts, weaving individual threads into communal tapestry of God's faithfulness. Written memoirs extend reach, allowing future generations to borrow courage. Digital platforms broadcast micro-stories—a brief post of God's provision for rent or peace in chemotherapy—multiplying praise across continents. Testimonies function apologetically, offering skeptics lived evidence of sustaining grace. They also correct survivor bias, acknowledging scars and setbacks while exalting preserving power. Hearing how others were kept reminds doubters that the same Shepherd walks their valley too (Ps 23:4).

9.10.3 Eternal security igniting present praise

Knowing that final salvation is secure does not breed complacency but detonates gratitude that reverberates through disciplines, relationships, and mission. Eternal security frees worshipers from anxious self-focus, releasing energy to adore Father, Son, and Spirit with undivided hearts. Songs of assurance—"He Will Hold Me Fast," "Blessed Assurance"—rise from pews with palpable relief. Secure saints give generously; money loses tyranny when future inheritance is guaranteed (Heb 10:34). They witness boldly; reputational risk shrinks compared to everlasting honor. Their homes radiate peace, for conflicts resolve under the banner of shared destiny. Security also braces for martyrdom: believers in hostile regions sing hymns en route to imprisonment, convinced death merely transitions them into promised glory (Phil 1:21). The doctrine thus proves intensely practical, transforming quiet devotions and public activism alike. Corporate liturgies that intertwine confession of sin with declaration of pardon model how security fuels ongoing repentance. As the final Amen echoes, the doxological life spills into streets, offices, and fields, advertising the keeping God to a restless world.

Conclusion

The testimony of Scripture and history is unanimous: God keeps His people, and His people keep going. Perseverance is therefore both gift and calling—an anthem of confidence in divine faithfulness and a summons to disciplined, hope-filled endurance. When doubts assail, promises anchor; when strength wanes, the Spirit renews; when the path grows dark, the lamp of future glory lights each step. Thus every sustained prayer, resisted temptation, and restored wanderer becomes a living doxology, proclaiming that "He who began a good work" will indeed bring it to completion (Phil 1:6). With hearts fortified by this assurance, we turn to the climax of salvation's story—glorification—where the race will give way to rest and perseverance will blossom into perfect, everlasting joy.

Chapter 10. Shall Be Saved: Glorification at the Lord's Appearing

The gospel story does not culminate in the grave, nor even in the ongoing transformation of sanctification; it surges toward a breathtaking horizon where faith turns to sight and every fragment of redemption reaches full bloom. Scripture calls this moment "glorification"—the instant the risen Christ appears, raises His people in incorruptible bodies, and unveils a remade creation free of death, decay, and sorrow. Long-nurtured promises become tangible realities: mortality is swallowed by life, justice is rendered without remainder, and the redeemed behold their God face-to-face in unbroken delight. This chapter traces that climactic future, not as distant speculation, but as the sure anchor that steadies present holiness, energizes mission, and re-interprets every affliction as preparatory glory.

10.1 The Promise of Final Salvation—Already / Not Yet

10.1.1 Spirit-sealed pledge of completion

The Holy Spirit's indwelling does more than comfort believers in the present; He functions as a legal earnest that obligates God to finish what He started (Eph 1:13-14). Every time the Spirit convicts of sin, assures of pardon, or stirs up worship, He whispers, "This is only the down payment." His ongoing work therefore anchors hope in objective covenant, not in shifting feelings or circumstances. The Spirit's seal is invisible to the naked eye, yet it exerts practical force: it restrains apostasy, awakens perseverance, and fosters holy longing. By tying future glory to present experience, the Spirit bridges epochs—making the world to come feel near even as it tarries. He also safeguards inheritance; no spiritual thief can breach God's vault because the pledge itself is divine power. This certainty fuels missionary risk, for those guaranteed tomorrow can expend themselves today without fear of ultimate loss. The seal likewise reframes suffering: groans within remind saints that the warranty will one day eliminate all repair work. When doubt arises, believers trace the signature of the seal by reviewing Spirit-wrought fruit—repentance, love, and resilience—not as grounds for pride but as evidence of ownership. In corporate worship the Spirit's presence intensifies anticipation, for collective praise amplifies the echo of future choirs. Baptism and Communion become seal-reinforcing dramas, tangible reassurances that the transaction is legitimate. Pastors therefore teach pneumatology not merely as doctrine but as eschatological counseling, equipping saints to lean into the pledge when storms threaten hope.

10.1.2 Creation's groaning and believer's eager waiting

Paul personifies the cosmos as a laboring mother, groaning for liberation from decay (Rom 8:19-22). Earthquakes, wilted flowers, and aging bodies form an orchestral lament that something better is coming. Believers join the chorus, groaning inwardly as they await adoption's fullness—the redemption of their bodies (Rom 8:23). Yet Christian groaning is uniquely hopeful; it knows the contractions herald birth, not death. The Spirit translates these sighs into intercession, aligning human ache with divine timetable. Environmental stewardship becomes an eschatological protest sign, declaring that creation's destiny is renewal, not disposal. Liturgy gives voice to groaning through psalms of lament, refusing triumphalism while rejecting despair. This waiting sharpens discernment: temporary pleasures lose luster when compared with imminent glory. Suffering gains context as "light and momentary," not by minimizing pain but by maximizing future weight (2 Cor 4:17). Mission expands, for a groaning creation longs to hear the liberating gospel; evangelism thus becomes midwifery for new-birth cosmos. Families teach children to interpret storms and sunsets as reminders that the world is in labor. Science and faith converge here: the laws of entropy echo Paul's theology, confirming that decay demands divine reversal.

10.1.3 Christ the firstfruits guaranteeing the full harvest

Jesus' resurrection is not an isolated miracle but the first sheaf waved before God to guarantee an entire harvest of redeemed humanity (1 Cor 15:20-23). Agricultural imagery assures agrarian and urban readers alike that God never begins without finishing. Firstfruits theology undermines fatalism: history is linear, moving from prototype to plenitude, not in endless cycles of despair. Every Christian burial plots a seed, confident that germination will occur at the trumpet's blast. This guarantee reshapes grief; we mourn, but as farmers lamenting winter loss while expecting spring yield. Christ's glorified body previews our own—recognizable yet radiant, physical yet incorruptible. His ascension, far from departure, is an advance claim on heavenly real estate for all united to Him. Firstfruits logic also fuels ethical harvest; if bodies will rise, what we do with them now—purity, service, suffering—matters eternally. Corporate worship on Resurrection Sunday is therefore both retrospective celebration and prospective rehearsal, a communal waving of future sheaves. Because the harvest is certain, the church sows gospel seed indiscriminately, trusting God for increase.

With the pledge secured, the groans interpreted, and the firstfruits displayed, attention now turns from promise to physiology: what will those harvested lives actually look like when the Lord appears?

10.2 Resurrection Bodies: Incorruptible & Immortal

10.2.1 "Sown perishable, raised imperishable" — nature of the glorified body

Paul contrasts present frailty with future splendor using four antithetical pairs: perishable/imperishable, dishonor/glory, weakness/power, natural/spiritual (1 Cor 15:42-44). "Spiritual" here means Spirit-animated, not ghost-like; glorified bodies will be as solid as Christ's post-Easter frame that broke bread and bore scars. Imperishability indicates immunity to disease, decay, and disability—wheelchairs, chemo, and glasses will reside only in museum exhibits of bygone sorrow. Glory refers to radiant beauty—bodies that refract divine brilliance like prisms, yet without sunburn or arrogance. Power signifies vigor unhampered by fatigue; marathon worship sessions will require no caffeine. The spiritual dimension implies perfect alignment between body and Spirit, ending the civil war between fleshly impulses and redeemed will. Memory will be healed: shameful scenes absorbed into redemptive testimony, no longer triggering guilt. Sensory capacities may be heightened—perhaps new colors perceived, or music resonating in dimensions now inaccessible. Yet continuity persists; personal identity survives, ensuring reunion recognitions and fulfilled vocations. The miracle is not annihilation of matter but its emancipation, enabling creation to fulfill its original design in Edenic harmony.

10.2.2 Continuity and discontinuity with present biology

Glorification retains fingerprints while removing fractures; thus resurrected bodies are both "us" and "new." Continuity preserves relational bridges—friends knew the risen Jesus by voice and mannerisms (John 20:16). Discontinuity appears when He passes through locked doors, hinting at physics upgraded rather than suspended (John 20:19). Our genetic heritage will likely persist—tribal diversity in Revelation suggests recognizable ethnic beauty (Rev 7:9). Yet age and infirmity will vanish; infants lost in tragedy may mature to optimal stature, elders regain youthful zest while retaining wisdom. Sexual complementarity endures without marriage's exclusivity, redirecting intimacy toward communal fellowship (Matt 22:30). Dietary continuity surfaces as Jesus eats fish, but dependence on food for survival may cease, converting meals into pure celebration (Luke 24:42-43). Blood chemistry will be transformed—no more pathogens, inflammation, or hormonal imbalance. Athletic potential may reach Edenic benchmarks—unfallen biomechanics free from injury. Artistic and scientific creativity will flourish, no longer hindered by cognitive decline or sinful rivalry.

10.2.3 Patterned after Christ's own resurrection appearance

Christ is prototype and architect of glorified humanity; studying His forty post-resurrection days yields clues. He greets disciples with "peace," indicating emotional equilibrium anchored in victory, not denial of prior pain (John 20:21). He invites touch—tactile reality dispelling ghost theories (Luke 24:39). He retains scars, transforming wounds into windows of grace; our scars likewise may narrate redemption rather than shame. His mobility transcends geographic limitation, appearing in Galilee and Jerusalem effortlessly; believers may experience similar freedom, enabling uninhibited exploration of renewed cosmos. Christ's conversations include Scripture exposition, hinting at ongoing theological discovery without error or debate fatigue (Luke 24:27). His commission signals purposeful activity; heaven's leisure is industrious delight, not eternal idleness. Therefore, glorified bodies will serve, create, and govern under King Jesus' delegated authority.

If individual bodies are slated for dramatic renewal, creation itself cannot remain static. The resurrection of people heralds the rebirth of planets and ecosystems—the theater of glory now takes its stellar turn.

10.3 Cosmic Renewal: New Heavens & New Earth

10.3.1 Creation liberated from bondage to decay

Paul envisions the entire cosmos erupting into freedom when God's children are revealed (Rom 8:21). This liberation is not annihilation; "new" denotes qualitative transformation, like "new covenant" built upon fulfilled promise. Entropy's relentless march will reverse—no rust, rot, or cosmic death spirals. Earthquakes will stabilize, viruses will retire, deserts may burst into bloom fulfilling Isaiah's foretaste (Isa 35:1). Animal predation ceases; Isaiah imagines wolves and lambs sharing pastures under carnivorous truce (Isa 11:6-9). Stellar realms likewise regenerate—supernovae halted, radiation balanced, cosmic background noise retuned to symphonic praise. Technology may integrate seamlessly with nature, untainted by exploitative extraction. Every "very good" potential suppressed by sin will blossom unhindered, fulfilling God's original commission.

10.3.2 Cultural treasures redeemed and brought into the city

John pictures kings bringing the glory and honor of the nations into the New Jerusalem (Rev 21:24-26). Far from cultural homogenization, eternity will showcase sanctified diversity— Szechuan spices, Yoruba rhythms, Incan textiles, Baroque architecture—purged of idolatry and infused with Christ-magnifying excellence. Nations' distinct languages may remain, now mutually intelligible by Spirit-enabled comprehension, preserving nuance without division. Artistic masterpieces lost to war or decay could be restored, or new creations surpass earthly peers without copyright squabbles. Economic exchange transforms from competitive capitalism or coercive communism into gift-based abundance—trade as celebration of others' craftsmanship. Scholarly disciplines flourish; mathematicians explore infinite patterns without fatigue, historians study untampered archives, physicists probe redeemed quantum realms. Festivals populate the cosmic calendar, each ethnicity hosting feasts that others eagerly attend, embodying gospel hospitality on planetary scale.

10.3.3 Ecological and vocational implications of a restored cosmos

A healed earth redefines vocation; gardeners, engineers, and poets discover unending projects aligned with divine mandate to cultivate and care (Gen 2:15). Environmental science becomes worship as researchers steward ecosystems that reciprocate in fruitful harmony. Agriculture loses weeds yet retains experimentation—crossbreeding flowers for sheer beauty rather than yield under curse. Architects design without zoning corruption; musicians compose knowing sound waves travel undistorted. Governance shifts from power consolidation to servant oversight, mirroring the Lamb's reign. Education abolishes ignorance but not learning; every discovery unveils fresh layers of God's wisdom (Eph 3:10). Physical exercise persists out of delight, not body-image anxiety; climbers scale peaks without peril, divers explore reefs unmarred by bleaching. Pets may remain companions under perfect stewardship, reflecting humanity's dominion redeemed.

With cosmos and culture transformed, justice must be publicly established. The stage is set for the final assize where every deed is weighed and every verdict vindicates the King's righteousness.

10.4 The Final Judgment: Perfect Justice & Joyful Vindication

10.4.1 Great white throne and books opened

John's vision places heaven and earth fleeing as the Judge takes His seat, signaling that no jurisdiction outranks this court (Rev 20:11-12). The opened books contain exhaustive records—thoughts, words, hidden motives—rendering defense attorneys obsolete. Judgment's transparency silences protests of unfairness; omniscient evidence precludes mistrials. Every systemic injustice—unpaid wages, silenced abuse survivors, genocides—faces divine scrutiny, assuring victims that their pain was logged, not overlooked. For the unredeemed, this disclosure precedes righteous sentence; for believers, another document—the Lamb's Book of Life—trumps charges with Christ's righteousness. The event magnifies God's attributes: holiness in sentencing evil, mercy in acquitting the justified, wisdom in perfect verdicts. Angels and humans agree: "True and just are Your judgments."

10.4.2 Bema seat—believers' works tested and rewarded

Paul distinguishes punitive judgment from the believer's evaluative tribunal, likening it to fire testing building materials (1 Cor 3:12-15). Gold, silver, and precious stones—acts done in faith—survive, becoming treasured rewards. Wood, hay, and straw—self-aggrandizing deeds—burn, leaving the worker saved yet impoverished. Rewards may include expanded stewardship, radiant crowns, and deeper capacities for joy. The assessment cultivates accountability; mundane tasks assume eternal significance when done unto the Lord. Motive scrutiny fosters humility; secret prayers may shine brighter than public platforms. Anticipation of reward kindles diligence without anxiety, for salvation is secure even if rewards diminish.

10.4.3 Public exoneration of God's righteousness and His people

Judgment day publicly vindicates God's justice and the faith of His children (Matt 25:31-40). Martyrs who seemed cursed will hear divine applause; slandered believers will be cleared before former accusers. Conversely, hypocritical religiosity will be unmasked, proving God impartial. The cosmic gallery—angels, demons, nations—witnesses the verdicts, silencing accusations that God tolerates evil. Christ shares His "Well done" with servants who mirrored His compassion in feeding the hungry or visiting prisoners, dignifying acts often unnoticed on earth. This public dimension satisfies the moral intuition that justice must be seen to be complete. Vindication dissolves lingering shame, freeing saints to step into eternal celebration unburdened.

Once justice is satisfied and guilt erased, nothing hinders direct encounter with God Himself. The redeemed now behold the blazing center of glory—the beatific vision that transforms sight into likeness.

10.5 Beatific Vision: Seeing God Face to Face

10.5.1 "We shall be like Him, for we shall see Him as He is"

The apostle John explains the causal link between vision and transformation: beholding Christ instantly refashions believers into His glorious likeness (1 John 3:2-3). In that moment no veil remains—neither the veil of fallen flesh nor the veil of partial revelation—so the gaze is comprehensive and unhindered. The sight is not merely optic; it is participatory, drawing saints into the very beauty they behold, much as sunlight both illuminates and warms. This likeness encompasses moral purity, emotional harmony, and intellectual clarity, erasing every vestige of sin's distortion. Formerly faith clung to promises and love pursued an unseen Beloved; now faith becomes sight and love embraces its object without mediation. The terror that once drove Moses to hide behind a cleft yields to confident adoration, for redemption has equipped the redeemed to endure and enjoy unveiled glory. Vision also equalizes status—kings and servants stand shoulder to shoulder, captivated by the same Majesty. The experience forever severs the power of temptation, because nothing lesser can compete once the eyes drink the fountain of infinite worth. Every aesthetic yearning—music, art, nature—finds its consummation in the radiant face of Christ, the archetype of all beauty. Saints will never tire of this sight; the infinite perfections of God ensure that fresh facets dazzle eternally. Even now, meditating on this promised vision purifies conduct, for anticipation reorients priorities and refines motives. Thus the beatific encounter is both future destiny and present incentive, forming the hinge between suffering patience and perfected joy.

10.5.2 Fullness of knowledge and unbroken communion

Paul contrasts current knowledge in a foggy mirror with future clarity "face to face," promising full—yet not exhaustive—comprehension when perfection arrives (1 Cor 13:12). Glorification unlocks the intellect, removing cognitive limits caused by finitude and fallenness; questions deferred—about providence, science, history—receive luminous answers. This knowing is relational, not mere data acquisition; it flows within unbroken communion where every insight becomes a fresh doxology. Mind and heart operate in seamless harmony, eradicating the frustration of understanding truth while lagging in obedience. Prayer turns into direct conversation without distraction, and worship loses the gap between confession and practice. The Spirit continues as Teacher, yet now every lesson lands in fully responsive soil, yielding immediate fruit. Mutual knowledge flourishes too; glorified saints understand one another without suspicion, cultivating transparent fellowship that mirrors the Trinity's shared life. Miscommunication vanishes as words convey intent perfectly, ending quarrels birthed by misunderstanding. Learning never plateaus—God's infinitude means discovery stretches unendingly, but the process elicits astonishment, not fatigue. The sciences thrive as acts of worship, with new phenomena prompting choruses, "O the depth of the riches!" Ethical debates cease because divine judgments are universally manifest, aligning conscience with cosmic jurisprudence. Such plenary knowledge sets the stage for eternal rest, for anxiety born of uncertainty evaporates.

10.5.3 Eternal Sabbath rest and delight in the Trinity

Hebrews speaks of a "Sabbath-rest for the people of God," a state where toil's frustration is replaced by celebratory repose (Heb 4:9-11). Glorification ushers believers into that ceaseless yet dynamic rest, where energy is expended without exhaustion and labor is joy rather than survival. Rest here is relational—basking in the Father's approval, the Son's companionship, and the Spirit's ever-refreshing presence. It heals the micro-fractures of hurried living, finally aligning internal pace with eternal rhythms. Worship becomes effortless breathing; service flows without the drag of selfish motives. Time no longer tyrannizes—there are no deadlines, only opportunities to explore goodness. Creativity flourishes because failure carries no shame; mistakes serve as stepping-stones to deeper wonder. Physical relaxation coexists with purposeful action, like dancers sustained by music itself. Emotional rest emerges as perfect security banishes fear; no threat, loss, or regret can intrude. This Sabbath atmosphere permeates relationships, the environment, and even memory, which is cleansed of trauma's sting. Having traced the vision, knowledge, and rest that crown redemption, we now turn to the communal tapestry woven from millions of glorified lives.

10.6 Eternal Community: Fellowship of the Redeemed

10.6.1 Multinational worship—every tribe and tongue

John's panorama of an innumerable multitude clothed in white and singing before the throne confirms that ethnic and linguistic diversity are not temporary hurdles but eternal treasures (Rev 7:9-10). Accents once divided now harmonize, each language adding color to the anthem of the Lamb. Translation devices become obsolete as Spirit-enabled comprehension preserves linguistic uniqueness without confusion—Pentecost's miracle made permanent. Cultural art forms—drums, harps, flutes—blend into polyphonic splendor, illustrating that the gospel does not erase identity; it exalts it. Pilgrims from persecuted church contexts stand beside former oppressors, both transformed into worshipers, displaying reconciliation's apex. Festival calendars expand: Ethiopian coffee ceremonies, Korean hanbok dances, Brazilian rhythms—all devoted to Christ. The spectacle vindicates mission sacrifices—missionaries see fruit from seeds sown in tears, now rejoicing with harvested nations. Such worship embodies justice, for marginalized voices take center stage, reversing histories of silencing. The corporate anthem crescendos but never completes; new verses arise as fresh revelations of God ignite novel expressions.

10.6.2 Relationships purified—no more sorrow, offense, or division

God wipes away every tear, not by selective amnesia, but by resolving every relational fracture in the light of consummate love (Rev 21:4). Apologies offered on earth yet unreceived will finally meet full reconciliation; misunderstood motives will be clarified, and bitterness evaporated. Social hierarchies dissolve—status, wealth, and power lose meaning when glory equalizes worth. Friendship operates without jealousy; admiration of another's reward intensifies shared joy rather than envy. Humor flourishes absent sarcasm that wounds; laughter becomes pure celebration of shared delight. Community events run smoothly—no volunteers burn out, no committees feud over minor details. Meals involve sincere conversation undistracted by phone screens or insecurity. Memory retains story but sheds sting; testimonies of past offenses magnify grace without reopening wounds. Families fragmented by death reunite, yet loyalty expands beyond genetics to universal siblinghood. This relational shalom radiates outward, informing the re-creative tasks awaiting co-regents of the kingdom.

10.6.3 Co-reigning and meaningful service in the kingdom

The servants of God "will reign for ever and ever," indicating authority delegated to all redeemed, not a ruling elite (Rev 22:5). Co-reigning entails stewarding renewed creation—governing galaxies, composing policies that promote flourishing, exploring art and science under the King's agenda. Service is worshipful vocation—city planning, garden cultivation, festival organizing—with responsibilities matching gifts honed during earthly apprenticeship. Leadership carries no corruption; decisions spring from perfect wisdom, and subjects respond with joyful cooperation. Hierarchy resembles orchestra sections under one conductor—diverse roles producing harmonious output. Projects unfold without scarcity;

collaboration outpaces competition. Saints once limited by illness or oppression now unleash latent potential, their talents ripened through trial now freed for constructive enterprise. Progress is endless because God's creativity is inexhaustible; thus boredom becomes impossible. The co-reigning mandate embodies the original Edenic charge, culminating the narrative arc begun in Genesis.

Such vibrant community presupposes the total eviction of evil. Before the city's gates are secured, the dragon must be crushed and all darkness expelled—an agenda addressed in the next section.

10.7 The End of Evil: Satan Crushed & the Second Death

10.7.1 Final defeat of the dragon, beast, and false prophet

Revelation dramatizes evil as a hellish trinity—dragon, beast, and false prophet—each representing satanic hostility, corrupt power, and deceptive religion (Rev 20:10). Their final consignment to the lake of fire signifies irreversible defeat; they will never resurface in sequel or rebellion. The timing follows a brief release designed to expose residual allegiance to darkness, proving God's judgment universally just. Angels escort these foes to their doom; the redeemed witness and worship, liberated from stalking menace. This act fulfills Genesis 3:15's ancient promise—Eve's Seed crushing the serpent's head. Cosmic order stabilizes; creation exhales relief as oppressor chains are melted forever. The spectacle educates; it reveals sin's true trajectory and vindicates God's seeming slowness as patient mercy rather than impotence.

10.7.2 Nature and justice of everlasting punishment

Jesus speaks of "eternal fire prepared for the devil and his angels," extending its scope to unrepentant rebels who rejected life (Matt 25:46). Hell's duration mirrors heaven's— eternal—underscoring that moral rebellion carries infinite weight when measured against infinite holiness. Punishment is proportionate; varying degrees of accountability align with levels of revealed light (Luke 12:47-48). Far from divine overreaction, eternal separation confirms human dignity—choices made in time are honored in eternity. Imagery of darkness and flame communicates both isolation and torment; physical metaphors convey spiritual desolation. A perfected conscience will agree with the sentence, silencing suspicion of cosmic cruelty. The doctrine provokes sober gratitude among the saved and urgent compassion toward the lost.

10.7.3 Ethical and missional urgency born of eschatological soberness

Knowing the terror of the Lord, Paul persuades men (2 Cor 5:11). Likewise, eschatological soberness galvanizes mission: evangelism becomes rescue operations, not mere recruitment. Ethical seriousness emerges—holiness matters when judgment looms. The church confronts injustice because eternal destinies hinge on present choices; silence in the face of oppression betrays both victims and perpetrators. Discipleship emphasizes repentance and faith, refusing cheap grace that ignores coming wrath. Prayer gains fervor; intercession storms gates of hell on behalf of prodigals. Preachers balance comfort with warning, honoring Christ's pattern. Pastoral care steers doubters away from despair toward urgent trust. Eschatological teaching thus cultivates both tenderness and tenacity.

With evil abolished, creation secure, and saints enthroned, eternal life unfolds in worship-infused work. The concluding section paints daily rhythms of the age to come.

10.8 Liturgy of the Age to Come: Unending Worship & Work

10.8.1 Song of the Lamb and creative expressions of glory

Heaven's soundtrack centers on the "new song"—"Worthy is the Lamb who was slain"—yet its arrangements evolve as redeemed creativity amplifies praise (Rev 5:9-14). Musical genres expand beyond earthly categories; instruments unknown to us exploit acoustic properties of a curse-free universe. Visual arts flourish: luminescent murals, kinetic sculptures powered by river-of-life currents, celestial light shows choreographed by angelic engineers. Poetry captures nuances of grace previously inexpressible, each stanza unveiling fresh facets of divine beauty. Spontaneous worship erupts in city squares when discoveries in science or history spotlight God's wisdom. Liturgical seasons bloom, marking creation's anniversaries, redemption milestones, and new mercies. Participation is universal; even tone-deaf saints on earth now sing effortlessly, voices tuned by perfection. Every expression preserves Christ-centric focus, ensuring that creativity magnifies rather than distracts from the Throne.

10.8.2 Work as worship—cultivating the garden-city

The New Jerusalem merges garden and metropolis; a river nourishes trees whose leaves heal nations, while streets of gold denote structured civilization (Rev 22:1-2). Citizens engage in stewardship tasks— horticulture, environmental management, architectural expansion—continuing the Genesis mandate without thorns. Engineers design eco-friendly transport powered by kinetic praise, while chefs craft menus from fruit that energizes without excess. Scholars curate histories of redemption, enabling endless learning expeditions. Governance councils composed of glorified saints deliberate new projects, each proposal assessed for its capacity to manifest God's glory and neighbor's good. Economic models operate on abundance; trade is gift exchange, profit is communal joy. Play interweaves work— sporting events display resurrected agility, and victories prompt thanksgiving rather than rivalry. Children grow in wisdom without mischief, apprenticed by artisans who teach skills as acts of discipleship. All labor flows back into worship, echoing "holy to the Lord" inscribed on every tool (Zech 14:20-21).

Paul hints that in the coming ages God will show "the immeasurable riches of His grace" (Eph 2:7). Eternity therefore is not static bliss but exponential exploration. Mathematical theorems unfold in infinite series, each proof revealing new dimensions of divine order. Astrophysicists map galaxies newly accessible through resurrected travel, singing psalms beneath nebulae. Linguists uncover pre-Babel linguistic roots, reconstructing Edenic etymology. Theologians dive ever deeper into Trinitarian mysteries, yet each finding opens grander vistas, ensuring scholarship never hits ceiling. Friendships deepen without jealousy; learning is communal, discoveries spark festivals of shared wonder. Curiosity becomes worshipful hunger, forever satisfied yet forever growing. No fear haunts that novelty may end, for God's goodness is bottomless.

10.9 Living in Light of Glory: Present Holiness & Hope

10.9.1 Purifying ourselves because He is pure

The certain prospect of seeing Christ does not lull believers into complacency; it galvanizes moral vigilance because the character of the coming King sets the standard for the present citizen (1 John 3:3). Hope and holiness thus travel together: whenever the mind fixes on the Lord's appearing, the will instinctively reaches for practices that mirror His purity. Every act of confession is an anticipatory cleansing, refusing to let stains cling to garments destined for radiant white. Spiritual disciplines—Scripture meditation, fasting, and accountability—act as refinement furnaces, burning away attitudes that would appear grotesque in that unveiled light. This forward-looking ethics reshapes choices as mundane as entertainment and as weighty as career moves, for anything incompatible with the age to come becomes unthinkable in the age that is. Even speech patterns adjust; sarcasm that bites and flattery that manipulates wilt under the gaze of the One whose lips drip grace. Purity here is neither prudish withdrawal nor self-imposed asceticism; it is joyful alignment with realities that will soon dominate the universe. Small victories in secret thoughts become rehearsals for public glory, and setbacks become tutoring sessions in deeper dependence on grace. The local church functions as a training ground, where weekly corporate worship temporarily lifts the veil, reminding saints what normal will soon look like. Baptism anniversaries and Communion tables reinforce identity, declaring that future perfection has already claimed these imperfect bodies. Parents disciple children by connecting bedtime prayers to resurrection morning, teaching that teeth brushing and heart guarding both prepare for meeting the King. Older saints mentor younger believers, showing by seasoned obedience that long-term purity is possible, desirable, and sustainable. As this hope-fueled holiness takes root, the church becomes a living preview of the world to come, whetting appetites for the day when purity will be effortless because sin will be impossible.

10.9.2 Suffering reinterpreted as birth pangs of glory

Paul dares to label present afflictions "light and momentary" because he weighs them against an eternal weight of glory that they actually help produce (2 Cor 4:17). Suffering, then, is not a random interruption but a skilled midwife, ushering resurrection life through the narrow canal of adversity. When pain tightens its grip, believers remind themselves that contractions intensify right before delivery; the agony signals nearness, not abandonment. Chronic illness becomes an unwelcome tutor that nevertheless coaches the soul in patient endurance, forging muscles that will flex effortlessly in the coming kingdom. Persecution positions the believer to taste in microcosm what Christ endured, thereby heightening the sweetness of future vindication. Economic hardship loosens the claws of materialism, making heavenly treasure feel imminently practical rather than pious abstraction. Grief over bereavement transforms into pregnant anticipation; every cemetery visit rehearses the explosive moment when those plots burst open at the trumpet blast. Lament psalms supply the grammar for honest sorrow, refusing both denial and despair by anchoring tears to promise. Community support turns individual trial into shared pilgrimage, distributing weight so that no one collapses beneath the load. Testimonies of deliverance—whether temporal rescue or sustaining grace—stack like Ebenezer stones, each one a reminder that the God who helped will help again until help is obsolete. Even creation's groans—earthquakes, pandemics, ecological decay—sound different in this key; they become the symphony's minor movements that make the final major chord brighter. Thus suffering loses its power to embitter; it becomes compost that nourishes hope, enriching the soil for the seeds of glory already sown in the heart.

10.9.3 Mission galvanized by the certainty of consummation

When angels promised that the ascended Jesus would return "in the same way you saw Him go," the disciples did not retreat to a mountain to await the spectacle; they hurried into Jerusalem to preach repentance and forgiveness (Acts 1:11). Eschatological certainty ignites evangelistic urgency because the closing curtain is fixed even if the exact schedule is undisclosed. The knowledge that God delays judgment to allow more people to come to repentance (2 Pet 3:9) reframes every day as mercy space for gospel witness. Conversations at bus stops, board meetings, and backyard fences gain cosmic weight; seed-sowing words might become last invitations before eternity locks doors. Global missions thrive on this timeline awareness, compelling churches to allocate resources strategically so that unreached peoples hear before the sky splits. Justice initiatives likewise accelerate, for eschatology unmasks oppression as temporary yet intolerable, calling believers to anticipate kingdom equity in present systems. Discipleship includes training believers to explain hope with gentleness, coupling apologetics with acts of compassion that authenticate the message. The arts become prophetic galleries, painting the coming glory in pigments of beauty that intrigue seekers. Environmental stewardship morphs into pre-emptive participation in the earth's future renewal, demonstrating that Christians care about the stage God plans to keep. Even vocational excellence—coding software, crafting policies, parenting toddlers—turns missional when framed as preview samples of the restored order. Thus the certainty of consummation does not breed star-gazing idleness; it sends feet running, hands serving, and mouths proclaiming so that when the King arrives He finds lamps lit and fields white for harvest.

Hope-driven holiness, pain reinterpreted, and mission on fire all crescendo in one inevitable response: unending praise to the God who orchestrates and completes salvation. The closing doxology gathers every thread into a single tapestry of glory.

10.10 Eternal Doxology: "To Him Be Glory Forever"

10.10.1 Angelic and human chorus in perfect harmony

John hears "the voice of a great multitude" like roaring waters and rolling thunder, announcing the marriage supper of the Lamb (Rev 19:6-7). In that thunderous choir, angelic seraphim who never knew redemption blend seamlessly with humans who tasted grace, producing harmonies impossible in the present age. Perfect pitch and flawless rhythm characterize the anthem because sin's dissonance has been eradicated; even the least musical saint now contributes a note that enriches the symphony. Lyrics center on God's attributes displayed across history—holiness in judgment, love in atonement, wisdom in providence, power in resurrection. Each stanza unveils a new facet, prompting an eternally unfolding composition that never repeats yet never departs from Christological focus. Instruments surpass earthly imagination: perhaps nebulae pulse as pipe organs while redeemed atoms resonate like strings. Spatial acoustics in the New Jerusalem allow sound waves to carry without distortion, enveloping worshipers in surround-sound glory. Participation is active, not passive; worshipers improvise their own grateful refrains, and the Spirit weaves them into the larger score. Silence punctuates at climactic moments, the hush itself a form of adoration more eloquent than words. This chorus is not a scheduled event but the ambience of eternity, infusing every activity—study, work, fellowship—with melodic undercurrent. Such harmony vindicates creation's original design for worship and eradicates every cacophony caused by sin's rebellion.

10.10.2 All things summed up in Christ

Paul envisions the Father's cosmic plan "to unite all things in Christ, things in heaven and things on earth" (Eph 1:10). This summing-up is more than organizational tidiness; it is the alignment of every molecule, narrative, and vocation under the coherent lordship of Jesus. History's loose threads—unanswered prayers, unresolved tragedies, unexplained providences—are braided into a tapestry that spells "Wisdom" when seen from the vantage of glory. Scientific laws and artistic principles find their common denominator in the Logos through whom they were made. Social hierarchies reorder under His servant-king ethic; crowns are cast down, and authority is exercised only as delegated stewardship. Memory itself is reindexed around Christ; personal stories are retold with His grace as interpretive key, eliminating self-centered boasting. Even angelic hierarchies take cues from His incarnation, recognizing that greatness is measured by self-giving love. This cosmic Christ-centricity liberates the redeemed from provincial perspectives, drawing them into universal solidarity rooted in their Head. Every praise rises to Jesus and, in raising, glorifies the Father and radiates through the Spirit, completing Trinitarian circulation of love.

10.10.3 Invitation to readers—join the Spirit and the Bride in saying "Come"

The Bible ends not with a systematic summary but with an invitation: "The Spirit and the Bride say, 'Come'" (Rev 22:17). That imperative reverberates backward through every page of this chapter and book, beckoning readers to situate their personal stories within the greater eschatological narrative. Responding begins now: surrender to the Savior, cultivate holiness, embrace mission, and nurture hope—all practical ways of echoing that invitation. Those already secure in Christ participate by longing, interceding, and laboring so that others may join the chorus before the curtain falls. Daily prayers of "Maranatha" keep hearts tender, while acts of mercy extend foretastes of coming compassion. The table is still being set, seats remain unfilled, and the banquet doors stand ajar; evangelistic urgency thus flows from doxological delight. Ultimately, the invitation circles back to worship—every "Come, Lord Jesus" is itself an act of praise that magnifies the faithfulness of the One who promises, "Surely I am coming soon." When He does, the Spirit's work will reach consummation, the Bride will stand spotless, and the echo of that invitation will resolve into everlasting satisfaction.

Conclusion

When the last trumpet sounds, perseverance will give way to perfect rest, and the "already" and "not yet" of salvation will resolve in a resounding "now." The same grace that justified us and has been sanctifying us will robe us in immortality, sweep away every shadow of evil, and seat us at the marriage feast of the Lamb. From that first eternal morning onward, worship and meaningful service will mingle in an ever-expanding joy, and the universe itself will echo with praise to the One who "makes all things new." Until that unveiling, hope of glorification fuels resilient faith and bold witness; after it, hope will be fulfilled and love will never cease. Even now the Spirit and the Bride say, "Come," and the church waits—not with crossed arms, but with outstretched hands—sure that the One who promised is coming soon.

Chapter 11. Living Between the Times

Believers occupy a spiritual frontier—post-resurrection yet pre-return—where the kingdom has already broken in but has not yet banished every shadow. In that overlap of ages, tension is normal: we taste freedom while wrestling weakness, celebrate victories while lamenting injustice, and carry the down-payment of the Spirit while yearning for full inheritance. "Living between the times" therefore calls for a distinct posture: eyes fixed on the horizon, feet planted in ordinary soil, and hands busy with work that previews the world to come. This chapter explores how that posture shapes identity, rhythms, witness, ethics, and imagination, so the people of God can inhabit the present as faithful ambassadors of the future.

11.1 The Eschatological Tension: Already & Not Yet

11.1.1 Kingdom inaugurated—signs of new creation now

When Jesus announced that the kingdom of God had drawn near, He was not speaking in metaphors but heralding a regime change that had already breached the present order (Luke 17:20-21). Every healing, exorcism, and pardon He issued functioned as an invasion beachhead, proving that the age to come was pushing back the old dominion of sin and death. Pentecost amplified that invasion; tongues of fire and transformed disciples demonstrated that the Spirit had begun rewriting the human operating system (Acts 2:1-4). Today the same kingdom footprints appear whenever addictions lose their grip, enemies reconcile, or oppressed communities taste justice earlier than expected. These foretastes are not anomalies; they are earnest money on the full inheritance, tangible reminders that God's future is already interrupting the present. Even mundane faithfulness—balanced budgets, honest words, diapers changed in love—signals that Christ's rule has entered ordinary time. The sacraments reinforce this reality as believers ingest bread and wine sourced from the old creation yet charged with new-creation power. Kingdom presence also calibrates prayer: intercession is not wishful thinking but partnership with a reigning King who delights to accelerate His agenda. Missional ventures ride this inaugurated wave, expecting supernatural favor because the gospel is announcing what is already true in principle. Theologians describe this overlap as the "semi-realized eschatology" that saturates New-Testament witness; practitioners simply call it hope with skin on. Still, the palpable presence of God does not erase the aches of incompletion, prompting the church to lift its eyes toward consummation.

11.1.2 Kingdom consummated—longing for full redemption

Paul likens the church to creation's midwives, groaning alongside the earth for the full unveiling of adoption and the redemption of our bodies (Rom 8:23). Although resurrection power pulses in our veins, mortality remains, evidenced by funeral processions and oncology wards. Tears still etch cheeks, and governments still falter; every headline of war or scandal testifies that shalom has not finished its work. Far from contradicting kingdom reality, these gaps intensify longing, expanding the soul's capacity for future joy. The Spirit Himself fans this yearning, translating sighs too deep for words into intercession aligned with divine timetable (Rom 8:26-27). Lament worship services give voice to holy impatience, reminding congregations that sanctified discontent is a virtue, not a lack of faith. Missionaries sense this tension vividly: every conversion celebrated in one village magnifies sorrow for unreached neighbors farther upriver. Artists portray the "not yet" through dissonant chords and unresolved canvases that refuse to pretend all is well. Spiritual disciplines of fasting and waiting embody hunger for the banquet still to come, refusing to be satisfied with appetizers. Yet longing is not despair; it is the stretching of faith toward promised completion, like a runner leaning toward the tape. This hope sharpens ethical edges; knowing destiny, saints refuse shortcuts that vandalize future glory. Thus the ache for consummation propels the next theme: how to live productively between promise and patience without tearing the fabric of either.

11.1.3 Holding promise and patience in creative tension

Hebrews urges believers to show diligence so that hope "might not be sluggish," marrying perseverance and anticipation in a single exhortation (Heb 6:11-12). Promise without patience devolves into reckless triumphalism; patience without promise collapses into passive resignation. The Spirit teaches the church to braid these strands into a rope strong enough for exile. Daily life becomes a pendulum swing: hands planted in soil cultivating gardens that may outlast us, hearts lifted toward skies that could split before sunset. Churches rehearse this rhythm in liturgy—songs of victory paired with prayers of lament, sermons of already grace followed by benedictions of waiting peace. Personal devotions alternate between contemplative stillness and activist petition, echoing Mary who pondered and Martha who served. Spiritual mentors coach disciples to pace zeal:

sprinting seasons balanced by Sabbaths, activism checked by abiding. Community discernment further tempers extremes; prophetic voices challenge complacency, while pastoral voices soothe frantic haste. The resulting posture is neither escapist nor utopian but a faithful steadiness that smells like eternity and feels like fidelity. Such balanced disciples are ready to navigate complex loyalties between temporal systems and heavenly citizenship—the focus of our next section.

11.2 Dual Citizenship: Heaven's Colonies on Earth

11.2.1 Identity as expatriate ambassadors

Paul states bluntly that our citizenship is in heaven, locating primary allegiance in a realm currently invisible yet decisively real (Phil 3:20). Like expatriates posted abroad, believers adopt local customs insofar as they harmonize with home-country ethics, but their passports reveal a superior jurisdiction. Embassies symbolize this reality: every local church is a sovereign outpost where the King's language, values, and communal economy are practiced publicly. Ambassadors do not seek cultural isolation; they engage host societies to convey policies of reconciliation, holding out visas of grace to anyone who wants citizenship transfer (2 Cor 5:20). Identity documents include baptism certificates and Spirit-bearing fruit that authenticate diplomatic status. When earthly flags wave, believers salute with respect yet reserve ultimate salutation for Christ crucified and risen. Such identity supplies insulation against culture wars; allegiance to Jesus stabilizes souls buffeted by partisan tides. Expatriate status also reframes suffering: persecution becomes diplomatic pressure, not personal misfortune. It inspires confidence in prayerful lobbying of heaven's court for resources, direction, and protection. Healthy ambassadorship requires fluency in host-culture language and kingdom dialect, motivating theological education and cross-cultural learning. This grounded diplomacy inevitably surfaces conflicts of loyalty, addressed next.

11.2.2 Loyalty conflicts—Caesar, culture, and Christ

Peter instructs believers to honor the emperor yet fear God, sketching a hierarchy that occasionally collides (Acts 5:29; 1 Pet 2:17). Taxes may be rendered to Caesar, but conscience cannot be surrendered when edicts contradict the gospel. Historical precedents abound: midwives in Exodus defied Pharaoh's infanticide; early Christians refused imperial cult worship; modern dissidents challenge unjust regimes. Lesser yet frequent clashes occur when workplace norms celebrate greed, school curricula embed nihilism, or familial traditions condone superstition. Discernment is required to distinguish salvageable cultural elements from idolatrous core. Civil disobedience, when necessary, is marked by respectful speech, willingness to suffer legal consequences, and prayer for persecutors. Spiritual disciplines like fasting sharpen loyalty calibration, enabling believers to detect subtle compromises. Corporate solidarity fortifies resolve; isolation magnifies fear of marginalization. Teaching on church history provides blueprints for faithful dissent without anarchic chaos. Ultimately, loyalty conflicts test whether believers view Christ's lordship as theoretical or ultimate. Such tests drive the need for embodied allegiance, explored in the next subsection.

11.2.3 Practicing embodied allegiance through lifestyle choices

Paul exhorts the Colossians to set minds on things above while simultaneously instructing them to mortify earthly vices and cultivate virtues (Col 3:1-17). This dual orientation manifests in embodied practices that broadcast allegiance more loudly than slogans. Budget decisions reveal kingdom investment priorities; generosity to the poor declares treasure in heaven. Sexual integrity proclaims that bodies belong to a resurrected Lord, not appetites or advertising algorithms. Media consumption curated through a Philippians 4:8 filter testifies that imagination already anticipates purity of the age to come. Hospitality extended to immigrants mirrors God's welcome without border walls. Environmental habits—recycling, energy stewardship—announce confidence in earth's future renovation, not its disposable status. Voting, purchasing, and posting on social media become liturgical acts performed before an audience of One. Such everyday liturgies tutor desires, ensuring identity and loyalty remain congruent. Embodied allegiance, however, demands sustainable rhythms, which leads naturally to patterns of work and rest between the times.

11.3 Rhythms of Waiting: Restful Work & Working Rest

11.3.1 Six-and-one cadence—Sabbath as eschatological protest

The Sabbath command is not merely humanitarian rest; it is a prophetic sign that human worth is not measured by output (Ex 20:8-11). In a productivity-obsessed economy, ceasing from labor once a week declares faith in God's provision and foreshadows the ultimate Sabbath awaiting the people of God (Heb 4:9). Sabbath observance therefore critiques oppressive systems that grind laborers for endless profit, aligning believers with slaves liberated from Pharaoh's quotas. Practices include digital detoxes, communal worship, leisurely meals, and creative hobbies undertaken without focus on monetization. Families prepare beforehand, mirroring Israel's collection of double manna, so rest is proactive, not merely collapsed exhaustion. Sabbath shapes identity: instead of saying "I produce, therefore I am," believers affirm "I am beloved, therefore I can rest." Over months, this rhythm recalibrates adrenalized bodies, easing anxiety and sharpening spiritual perception. It also cultivates joyful anticipation; if one day of delight feels this good, how marvelous eternal rest will be.

11.3.2 Vocation as cultivation of foretaste gardens

Jeremiah's counsel to exiles—plant gardens, build houses, raise families—models how vocational faithfulness seeds foretastes of the future city even in foreign soil (Jer 29:5-7). Work becomes continuation of Edenic stewardship, anticipating the garden-city of Revelation. Educators shape imaginations, engineers solve creational puzzles, and entrepreneurs generate goods that bless neighbors. Excellence signifies that the King cares about quality; integrity signals that hidden work is still holy. Mentoring younger colleagues forms a chain of vocational discipleship, ensuring kingdom values outlast one generation. Workplace prayer groups intercede for corporate ethics and employee well-being, translating spiritual authority into tangible culture shifts. Sabbatical leaves and professional development are pursued not for résumé polish but for increased capacity to serve. Failure, inevitable in vocational endeavor, is reframed as apprenticeship, echoing resurrection logic that life springs from apparent loss. Thus labor itself becomes liturgy, leading seamlessly to the interplay of leisure and industry.

11.3.3 Holy leisure and hopeful industry held together

Ecclesiastes affirms that it is God's gift to enjoy one's toil and the fruit of that toil (Ecc 3:11-13). Leisure, then, is not escape from calling but complementary celebration of it. Reading fiction, hiking mountains, or painting landscapes cultivate capacities for wonder that fuel creativity back at the desk. Shared recreation fosters community bonding, enabling gospel hospitality around grills and board games. Leisure practiced with gratitude inoculates against idolatrous binge-pleasure that leaves souls emptier. Conversely, industry devoid of periodic play becomes Pharaoh's brick factory, producing cynical slaves. A calibrated rhythm—morning labor, evening laughter; intense seasons of output followed by vacation retreat—mirrors planting and harvest cycles embedded in creation. The Spirit guides discernment: some seasons demand strategic hustle, others command deliberate slow-down. Honoring both keeps hope tactile and witness credible, positioning believers to engage culture without burnout, which is the heartbeat of the next section.

11.4 Public Witness: Culture-Making & Prophetic Dissent

11.4.1 Common-grace partnerships for societal good

Jeremiah urged exiles to seek the peace of Babylon, revealing that gospel people can collaborate with unbelievers on projects promoting human flourishing (Jer 29:7). Christians join city councils, environmental coalitions, or medical research teams, leveraging shared values for the common good. Such alliances require theological humility: recognizing that divine truth often seeps into secular conscience via common grace. Projects—clean-water initiatives, literacy campaigns, affordable housing—become staging grounds where kingdom ethics shine in cooperative deeds. Participants maintain integrity by openly crediting motivation to Christ while respecting pluralistic frameworks. Success breeds credibility, softening soil for explicit evangelism and demonstrating that Christian hope yields practical benefits now.

11.4.2 Prophetic confrontation of idolatrous systems

While cooperating for good, the church must also expose idols—materialism, nationalism, racial supremacy—that enslave societies (Mic 6:8). Prophetic dissent employs truth-telling speech seasoned with tears, refusing both hateful rhetoric and silent complicity. Historical models include Wilberforce confronting the slave trade and modern advocates challenging consumer injustice. Prophets analyze root narratives—what false promises sustain exploitation—and counter them with kingdom narratives of dignity and sufficiency. Activism extends beyond petitions to embodied alternatives: fair-trade purchasing, inclusive worship, interracial friendships. Costly obedience may provoke backlash, mirroring earlier saints who faced lions or lynch mobs. Yet persecution authenticates message, revealing allegiance to a higher throne.

11.4.3 Creative presence—art, technology, scholarship as kingdom signposts

Jesus labeled His followers the light of the world, implying visibility in public domains (Matt 5:14-16). Artists craft beauty that whispers of transcendent order; painters render lament and hope on canvases, composers write symphonies that resolve dissonance into harmony. Technologists design apps that foster community rather than addiction, demonstrating redemptive innovation. Scholars publish research integrating faith and intellect, challenging dogmatic secularism and lazy anti-intellectualism within the church. Twitter threads and TikTok reels become micro-parables when stewarded with originality and humility. This creative presence avoids preachy propaganda; it invites curiosity and dialogue. Over time, culture observers note patterns of life-giving contribution traced back to people who claim citizenship in another kingdom. Such resonance turns hearts toward the source of light, closing the circle back to the inaugurated kingdom glimpsed in section 11.1 and setting the stage for deeper exploration of ethics and mercy beyond this portion of the chapter.

11.5 Ethics Between Ages: Holiness, Justice, & Mercy

11.5.1 Personal holiness amid moral flux

A culture caught in relativism often treats moral convictions like fashion trends—discarded when inconvenient—but Peter insists exiles must pattern their conduct after the unchanging character of the Holy One (1 Pet 1:14-16). Holiness in this in-between era refuses both isolation and assimilation; it is separation *unto* God, not withdrawal *from* neighbors. Concretely, that means resisting the temptation to bend sexual ethics to social norms, guarding honesty when workplace incentives reward half-truths, and cultivating speech that heals rather than scorches in an age of outrage. The Spirit employs ordinary means—Scripture, confession, community accountability—to sand away habits of envy and covert self-promotion. Holiness flourishes when believers remember that their bodies are early installments of glorified temples and that every moral choice previews resurrection quality control. Because legalism stalks any conversation on purity, the gospel must daily remind saints that identity precedes behavior; obedience is a response to belovedness, not a down payment on it. When failures occur, swift repentance keeps shame from ossifying into cynicism, converting stumbles into stepping-stones of deeper grace. Households practice holiness by turning dinner tables into micro-sanctuaries of prayer, laughter, and candid repentance, modeling to children that godliness is both serious and joy-soaked. Technology audits—setting screen limits, curating playlists—translate holiness into digital environments, testifying that Christ's lordship extends to pixels and hashtags. Vocational integrity—refusing bloated invoices, honoring commitments—evangelizes colleagues who trust character before creeds. Such personal holiness, though seemingly private, carries public weight, preparing disciples to engage systemic brokenness with credible voices, as explored in the justice subsection next.

11.5.2 Pursuing justice from a grace-formed heart

Micah's triad—"do justice, love mercy, walk humbly" (Mic 6:8)—anchors activism in worship, ensuring zeal operates within grace rather than self-righteous fury. Justice between the times acknowledges partial victories: prison reform bills may pass while racial wounds still bleed, yet each reform is a kingdom seed that signals the soil is softening. Grace-formed advocates listen before speaking, recognizing that lament precedes strategy and that stories shape policies. They resist tribal echo chambers, drawing wisdom from diverse voices without diluting biblical categories of dignity. Prayer walks around city halls tether civic action to spiritual dependence, and fasting days sensitize hearts to the hunger statistics activists quote. Economic justice begins in local churches through fair wages for staff, transparent budgets, and micro-loan initiatives that honor entrepreneurial image-bearers. Internationally, believers leverage global supply chains—choosing ethically sourced goods—to protest exploitation with

197

purchasing power. The cross forbids both despair and triumphalism: Christ's finished work guarantees ultimate equity, yet His ongoing intercession calls saints to stand in gaps until that day. Justice pursued in this posture avoids the pitfalls of utopianism or nihilism, embodying a patient urgency seasoned with compassion. As campaigns meet resistance, activists recall that resurrection erupted after apparent defeat, fueling perseverance. That resilience merges seamlessly with mercy ministries, which translate justice into personalized compassion, our next focus.

11.5.3 Mercy ministries as previews of coming shalom

Jesus' parable of the Good Samaritan redefines neighbor love as hands-on mercy that bridges ethnic, economic, and religious divides (Luke 10:36-37). In the overlap of ages, soup kitchens, refugee housing, and addiction recovery centers operate as prototypes of the healed society Isaiah envisioned. Volunteers greet trauma survivors by name, offering dignity long denied, and in doing so rehearse the heavenly welcome awaiting all redeemed. Mercy work refuses savior complexes by partnering with recipients, recognizing mutual need and shared image-bearing worth. Churches adopt "benevolence budgets" that prioritize long-term empowerment—job training, financial counseling—over temporary relief, echoing Jesus' holistic healings that restored both body and social standing. Hospitality extends mercy into living rooms, converting spare bedrooms into sanctuaries for students and single parents. Short-term mission trips shift from photo-ops to skill-transfer residencies, equipping local leaders to outlast visiting teams. Mercy also includes advocacy for policy changes that address root causes—predatory lending, food deserts—so compassion tackles both symptoms and systems. Storytelling events let beneficiaries narrate their own journeys, fostering empathy that statistics cannot. As mercy ministries proliferate, they cultivate communities resilient in suffering, a reality explored in the next section on pilgrim endurance.

11.6 Pilgrim Suffering: Lament, Resilience, & Joy

11.6.1 Biblical lament giving voice to exile ache

Psalm-writers teach exiles to pray raw—"How long, O Lord?"—without slipping into blasphemy or bitterness (Ps 42; Ps 13). Lament insists that grief be spoken, not stuffed, because silence breeds cynical detachment. Congregational lament services weave minor-key hymns, testimonies of loss, and responsive readings to normalize honest sorrow within faith communities. Journaling laments at home complements public lament, mapping inner turbulence for divine review. Lament theology distinguishes complaint *to* God from complaint *about* God, maintaining covenant intimacy even when providence feels puzzling. Educators train youth to lament global tragedies—school shootings, refugee crises— so empathy matures early. Artists express communal ache through murals and spoken word, giving urban neighborhoods a vocabulary for collective wounds. Lament also tempers triumphalist impulses in worship sets that skip too quickly to victory, honoring the already/not-yet tension. By verbalizing pain, lament clears emotional debris, readying hearts for seeds of resilience to sprout, which the next subsection addresses.

11.6.2 Resilience forged in temporal affliction

Paul's catalogue of hardships—shipwrecks, lashes, hunger— culminates in an uncrushed spirit because grace supplies inner reinforcement (2 Cor 4:8-9). Modern resilience strategies echo but cannot surpass this heavenly fortification: cognitive reframing aligns thoughts with gospel truths; communal support mirrors body-part interdependence; spiritual disciplines anchor identity beyond circumstances. Survivors of persecution report that memorized Scripture passages became portable refuge when Bibles were confiscated. Trauma-informed pastoral care helps sufferers process flashbacks, integrating neuroscience with Spirit-empowered comfort. Physical practices—exercise, sleep discipline—support resilience by honoring embodied creaturehood. Story-sharing circles enable collective resilience as victories and relapses are narrated without stigma. When resilience matures, it resists both stoic suppression and fragile avoidance, embodying a rugged hope that expects joy to coexist with scars. Such paradoxical joy, our next focus, crowns the pilgrim path.

11.6.3 Paradoxical joy fueled by future inheritance

James' call to "count it all joy" in trials is not masochism but forward-looking math: loss now plus glory later equals surplus joy (Jas 1:2-4). This joy surfaces in prison hymns, chemo-room humor, and refugee camp choirs—songs that confound onlookers yet authenticate the gospel's power. Future inheritance acts like compound interest; the longer trials persist, the richer the coming yield, amplifying rejoicing. Joy strengthens perseverance muscles, creating a virtuous spiral: delight empowers obedience, obedience deepens delight. Feasting amid hardship—celebratory meals even on tight budgets—tangibly enacts joy, proclaiming that scarcity cannot strangle gladness. Corporate worship positions lament and joy as dance partners, transitioning from minor lament to major praise within the same service. Spiritual mentors caution that joy is not constant mood elevation but settled confidence in God's unwavering good. This settled confidence frees imagination to paint vibrant pictures of redemption, segueing to the next section on hopeful creativity.

11.7 Hopeful Imagination: Story, Beauty, & Creation Care

11.7.1 Gospel-shaped storytelling countering dystopia

In a media landscape flooded with apocalyptic doom, believers craft narratives where darkness is real yet resurrection has the last word (Rev 12:11). Christian novelists write speculative fiction featuring redeemed AI or reconciled ecosystems, challenging inevitability of collapse. Parents read children Bible-based adventure tales that celebrate courage and sacrifice, shaping moral imagination before cynicism encroaches. Testimony nights serve as live storytelling labs, where ordinary saints recount God's interventions, offering plot arcs truer than fictional heroics. Film clubs critique blockbusters through hope lenses, discerning echoes of redemption in unlikely places. Seminaries teach homiletics that employ narrative tension, climax, and resolution, making sermons pulsing stories rather than data dumps. Social media storytellers share micro-parables—threads that spotlight kindness in city corners—countering algorithm-amplified outrage. These stories inoculate hearts against despair, proving the future can be bright without denying current shadows.

11.7.2 Aesthetics that echo the splendor to come

Bezalel's Spirit-filled craftsmanship in Exodus validates artistic vocation as divine calling (Ex 31:2-5). Painters, graphic designers, and architects pursue excellence not for self-promotion but to anticipate the beauty of New Jerusalem's jeweled walls. Church sanctuaries commission local artists to depict biblical panoramas in contemporary styles, preaching through pigment. Fashion designers reject exploitative fast-fashion cycles, producing garments that honor the body as temple. Photographers highlight unnoticed wonder—dew on spiderwebs, wrinkles of aged hands—training viewers to recognize glory in the commonplace. Musicians incorporate global scales and instruments, anticipating transnational worship, while choreographers choreograph liturgical dances that fuse lament and hope. Gardens around church campuses become living art, integrating pollinator habitats with meditative pathways. Beauty thus becomes evangelistic, provoking questions that facts alone rarely raise.

11.7.3 Stewardship of earth as rehearsal for cosmic renewal

Genesis places humanity in Eden not as exploiter but as guardian-artist, a role reaffirmed by Romans' promise that creation awaits our glorification (Gen 2:15; Rom 8:21). Recycling programs, carbon-footprint audits, and community gardens signal allegiance to that mandate. Outdoor liturgies on Earth Day frame environmental action as worship not ideology. Farmers in faith networks experiment with regenerative agriculture, healing soil and sequestering carbon while increasing yield. Tech entrepreneurs design solar micro-grids for villages off national power lines, merging innovation with compassion. Youth groups adopt river clean-ups, learning ecology alongside theology. The church's ecological fidelity offers prophetic critique to consumer culture, announcing that the planet is not disposable staging. As creation flourishes under responsible care, it sings psalms that fuel discernment, the topic of the next section.

11.8 Practices of Discernment: Prayer, Wisdom, & Waiting

11.8.1 Watchful prayer guarding hearts

Jesus' command "stay awake and pray" in Gethsemane was not only for apostles but for every disciple navigating end-time ambiguity (Mark 13:33; 14:38). Watchful prayer combines attentiveness to world events with surrendered trust, preventing both paranoia and apathy. Believers create prayer rhythms synced to news cycles—pausing doom-scrolling to intercede for nations rather than internalize anxiety. Breath prayers—"Lord, have mercy"—fit commute congestion and boardroom tension alike, recalibrating perspective. Journaling prayers capture discernment impressions, forming archives that reveal patterns of God's guidance. Corporate prayer nights employ listening segments where silence invites Spirit promptings tested against Scripture. Such vigilance detects subtle heart drift—envy cloaked as ambition, bitterness masquerading as discernment—correcting course before shipwreck.

11.8.2 Community wisdom for ambiguous times

Proverbs extols counsel's safety; in late-modern labyrinths, isolated decision-making courts disaster (Prov 15:22). Discernment teams—diverse in age, gender, background— evaluate opportunities and dilemmas through multi-angled lenses, seeking consensus shaped by Word and Spirit.

Churches host "wisdom forums" where professionals discuss ethics in AI, genetics, and finance, equipping saints for frontline complexity. House-church clusters practice communal Lectio Divina, trusting collective insight over charismatic individualism. Mentoring triads pair younger believers with seasoned guides, fostering dialogue that refines vocational direction. Digital platforms facilitate cross-cultural consultation, broadening perspective beyond local bias. When consensus eludes, communities practice "non-coercive waiting," acknowledging finitude and respecting conscience.

11.8.3 Holy patience versus anxious activism

Psalm 37 contrasts fretting with trusting, urging saints to dwell in the land and befriend faithfulness (Ps 37:7). Holy patience is not lethargy; it is strategic stillness that resists frantic activism incapable of measuring long-term impact. Sabbath margins create breathing room for reflection before launching new ministries. Leaders integrate sabbatical cycles into strategic plans, preventing vision from outrunning soul. Activists adopt "rhythms of resistance"—action seasons balanced by contemplation retreats—mirroring Jesus' pattern of withdrawal and engagement. Patience also tempers consumer impatience, enabling believers to invest in slow-bloom relationships rather than instant gratification. Waiting becomes a testimony to a hurried world that trust trumps control. Such poised discernment re-integrates with personal holiness, justice, mercy, and imagination, completing the toolkit for faithful living between resurrection dawn and eschatological noon.

11.9 Inter-Generational Discipleship & Kingdom Legacy

11.9.1 Older saints teaching perseverance

Paul urges Titus to enlist seasoned believers as tutors of steadfastness, charging gray-haired men and women to display dignity, self-control, and sound faith (Tit 2:2-5). Such mentoring counters a culture that idolizes youth and sidelines elders, reminding the church that wrinkles can be spiritual credentials. Veterans of faith narrate decades of answered prayer, failed ventures redeemed, and midnight crises met by sunrise mercies, offering living case studies of God's keeping power. Their stories anchor younger disciples who know theology but lack long mileage on rough roads. Practical wisdom flows in both directions: retirees teach margin and Sabbath to ambition-driven professionals, while receiving digital literacy or cultural updates in return. Shared projects— community gardens, prison-letter teams—turn abstract counsel into shoulder-to-shoulder apprenticeship. Elders model repentance, not perfection, showing how to confess with dignity and rise without self-loathing. Grandmothers host "story pies" nights where pastries accompany testimonies, sweetening doctrine with tangible hospitality. Grandfathers walk with teens, praying aloud on city sidewalks, normalizing conversational communion with God. By embodying courage in illness and grace in grief, older saints demystify suffering's valley, proving that the Shepherd's rod still guides in shadowed seasons. Local churches formalize these relationships with "Barnabas teams" that pair households across generations for quarterly meals and monthly check-ins. Seminar rooms become inter-age think tanks where business acumen meets missionary vision, forging strategies richer than mono-age ingenuity. As wisdom accumulates like fertilizer, younger leaders sprout resilient callings, convinced that faith can outlast cultural turbulence. This transfer of perseverance capital prepares the stage for youthful innovators to imagine fresh kingdom advances.

11.9.2 Youth envisioning fresh kingdom frontiers

Paul exhorts Timothy not to let anyone despise his youth but to set believers an example in speech, conduct, and purity (1 Tim 4:12). Young disciples possess cultural fluency, risk tolerance, and holy restlessness that can propel the gospel into unexplored spaces. Teen coders create apps that connect prayer partners across continents, gaming enthusiasts plant virtual Bible studies in MMORPG guilds, and college students launch micro-enterprises that hire refugee artisans at fair wages. When elders grant real responsibility—pulpit slots, budget lines, decision-making seats—youthful fervor matures into covenant faithfulness. Failures are expected; safe-to-fail environments let leaders experiment without catastrophic fallout, turning mistakes into masterclasses. Short-term mission internships morph into long-term cross-cultural vocations as young adults discover language learning capacities and relational adaptability. High-schoolers host climate forums from a biblical stewardship lens, reframing activism with eschatological hope rather than eco-despair. Music collectives write worship in emerging genres, engaging peers alienated by traditional forms yet hungry for transcendence. Social-media micro-evangelists share one-minute apologetics that seed curiosity in scroll-weary hearts. Youth councils interview civic leaders, advocating policies that protect the unborn and the marginalized alike, embodying integrated pro-life ethics. Mentoring relationships flip as twenty-somethings teach grandparents how to defend the faith on Instagram, turning screens into testimony stages. Momentum from these initiatives convinces the broader congregation that God delights to pour new wine into fresh skins, even while honoring vintage stock. Such synergy requires relational bridges—families and friendships—that continuously shuttle hope across age divides.

11.9.3 Families and friendships as transmission belts of hope

Moses commands parents to impress covenant words on children during walks, meals, and bedtime rituals, embedding faith in life's cadence (Deut 6:6-9). In the between-times, households function as micro-seminaries where creeds are recited at breakfast and forgiveness is practiced before sleep. Story Bibles at the dinner table cultivate theological literacy alongside table manners. Shared mission trips turn vacations into vision casting, bonding siblings through service rather than consumer entertainment. God-parents and church "aunties" widen the spiritual kinship web, ensuring no child navigates adolescence with only two adult voices. Friendship bands—singles, widows, couples—form intentional pods that rotate hosting responsibilities, demonstrating kingdom family to onlookers marked by loneliness epidemics. Rituals such as Advent wreath lighting, Passover-style Easter meals, and

Pentecost kite flying engrave salvation history on young imaginations far deeper than lecture could. Conflict-resolution charts posted on fridge doors guide quarrelling toddlers and tense spouses alike through confession and reconciliation steps, making peace-making muscle memory. Tech agreements limit screen intrusion during car rides, creating windows for spontaneous prayer or hymn humming. College departures trigger commissioning liturgies in living rooms, sending students as campus missionaries rather than anxious freshmen. Family giving jars collect coins for global outreach, teaching that allowances and inheritances are trust funds for kingdom expansion. As relational networks hum with such practices, legacy crystallizes: generation to generation will laud His works (Ps 145:4).

When age-spanning discipleship fashions persevering elders, visionary youth, and hope-infused households, the community is primed to cultivate daily rituals that keep anticipation of Christ's return vibrating in ordinary moments—the habits of "everyday Maranatha."

11.10 Everyday Maranatha: Habits of Anticipation

11.10.1 Greeting the day with "Come, Lord Jesus" expectancy

Each sunrise offers a liturgical prompt: before scrolling headlines or brewing coffee, believers whisper, "Even so, come" (Rev 22:20). This simple invocation reframes morning priorities—emails become opportunities for gospel clarity, commutes convert to intercessory walks, and calendars morph into strategic stewardship rather than tyrants. Some disciples set phone alarms at 12:00 and 6:00 p.m. labeled "Maranatha," pausing for thirty-second prayers that recalibrate midday and evening. Kitchen chalkboards carry the Aramaic phrase as household calligraphy, schooling children in eschatological vocabulary. Runners lace shoes imagining they might hear the real trumpet before reaching mile three, turning exercise into rehearsal for meeting the Lord in the air. Journal headers record daily longings and observable foretastes—sunrises, answered prayers, acts of justice—

training eyes to spot kingdom sprouts. Community groups open gatherings by articulating one specific sphere where they desire Christ's intervention that week—corporate boardroom ethics, neighborhood violence, chronic illness—and close by thanking Him in advance. This rhythm inoculates against apathy and fuels courage, priming hearts for tangible acts of kingdom investment like generosity.

11.10.2 Practicing generosity as future-treasure investing

Jesus links treasure location to heart orientation, inviting disciples to convert temporal assets into eternal yield (Matt 6:19-21). Practicing generosity therefore becomes an eschatological investment strategy: portfolios tilt toward missions, mercy, and art that will echo in the new creation's galleries. Couples budget a "second-coming line item," allocating funds each month to spontaneous Spirit nudges—grocery cards for single moms, tuition for refugees, seed money for church plants. Estate plans designate percentages for kingdom causes, signaling to heirs that wealth is baton, not security blanket. Minimalist wardrobes and shared tool libraries free up capital while protesting consumer idolatry. Generosity spills beyond money: spare bedrooms host international students; frequent-flyer miles transport missionaries on furlough; vacation days turn into disaster-relief deployments. Givers track stories, not just receipts, logging how resources catalyze salvations or systemic change, reinforcing joy that dwarfs stock-market swings. Such patterns expose mammon's emptiness and entice onlookers to a radically different economy governed by future audit.

11.10.3 Celebrating small foretastes—healings, reconciliations, justice wins— as down-payments on final glory

Acts portrays seasons of "refreshing" that prefigure cosmic restoration (Acts 3:19-21). Churches cultivate watchfulness by spotlighting micro-resurrections: cancer scans returning clear, estranged siblings hugging after years of silence, court rulings that protect the vulnerable. Testimony segments interrupt service scripts, allowing fresh victories to trigger spontaneous doxology. Social-media channels function as digital Ebenezer walls, archiving stories with hashtags like #foretasteFriday. Dinner parties toast answered prayers with sparkling juice, teaching tastebuds to associate sweetness with divine faithfulness. Artists sketch murals of local breakthroughs, embedding hope in neighborhood landscapes. When setbacks follow, communities revisit these archives, reminding each other that trajectory, not snapshot, defines the narrative. Small wins shape prayer requests—if God reversed that injustice, why not this one? Annual "foretaste festivals" invite ministry partners to share updates, turning donor banquets into worship extravaganzas. Recognizing down-payments protects from cynicism; it trains the soul to treat delays as purposeful pacing, not cancellation.

Conclusion

The space between Christ's triumph and His triumphal return is not an empty waiting room; it is the active theater where hope trains holiness, suffering forges resilience, and everyday choices become signposts of the new creation. When disciples embrace their dual citizenship—rooted in heaven, engaged on earth—they transform workplaces, neighborhoods, and cultures with foretastes of the age that is rushing toward us. Living this way stitches the gospel's three tenses into a single tapestry: once saved, now being saved, and soon to be gloriously saved. Until the King appears, we navigate the already/not-yet with watchful prayer, courageous love, and a steady "Maranatha" on our lips—confident that every faithful step taken in the twilight will blaze with significance at dawn.

Chapter 12. Conclusion: Embracing the Full Journey of Salvation

The sweep of redemption stretches from the instant God calls a sinner out of darkness to the endless ages when that saint shines with reflected glory in the presence of Christ. Along the way, grace announces three distinct yet inseparable tenses: we have been decisively saved from sin's penalty, we are continually being saved from sin's power, and we shall one day be fully saved from sin's presence. This concluding chapter gathers the threads spun through every prior page—justification's courtroom verdict, sanctification's daily apprenticeship, Spirit-empowered witness, corporate life in sacraments and mission, patient perseverance, and the promised unveiling of glory—and braids them into a single, unbreakable cord of hope. Its purpose is not to introduce new doctrine but to help readers step back, trace the contours of the whole canvas, and feel the gospel's full weight settle into mind, heart, and vocation.

12.1 Grasping the Three-Tense Gospel in One View

12.1.1 Saved Once for All: The Finished Work of Justification

The journey opens at a courtroom where the Judge of all declares the ungodly righteous because Another has borne their guilt (Rom 3:24-26). Justification is not God's lenient wink at sin but His public vindication of justice, displayed as He sets forth Christ as a propitiation. In that single verdict every indictment in heaven's docket is stamped "paid in full," freeing the conscience from its relentless prosecutor (Col 2:13-14). The transfer is instantaneous and irreversible; the believer can never be "more justified" tomorrow than today, for the status is perfect, complete, and grounded outside personal performance. Assurance flows from this objectivity: faith rests not on the volatility of emotion but on the unchanging accomplishment of Calvary. Because the righteousness credited is Christ's own, the Father delights in adopted children with the same affection He lavishes on His Son (John 17:23). This standing seeds humility; boasting is silenced because all glory belongs to the cross. It also seeds boldness; prayer rises unshrinking, for no sin remains to disqualify the petitioner (Heb 4:16). Celebrating justification each morning rewires identity, shrinking the power of failure and the seduction of applause. Baptism dramatizes this grace, marking the believer's passport as citizen of a kingdom secured by blood, not merit. Yet the story would be truncated if it ended at the gavel; the justified still inhabit unglorified bodies and unrenewed cultures. The verdict therefore becomes the launching pad for continual transformation, ushering us into the second tense of salvation.

12.1.2 Being Saved Daily: The Ongoing Work of Sanctification

Sanctification translates the courtroom decree into a lifetime apprenticeship under the Spirit's tutelage (2 Cor 3:18). Here the believer is both participant and recipient, working out salvation while God works within (Phil 2:12-13). Each dawn the Spirit opens a renovation site in the heart, targeting impatience in the school-run queue or cynicism in the board meeting. Scripture serves as blueprint, exposing structural cracks and sketching new patterns of mercy, purity, and courage (Ps 119:105). Trials become sanctifying chisels; friction with colleagues smooths rough pride, and lingering illness carves deeper dependence (Jas 1:2-4). Growth is rarely linear—two steps forward, one relapse—but grace transforms even backward slides into tutorials on deeper grace. Community accelerates progress: gentle rebukes keep blind spots from ossifying, and shared wins kindle corporate hope (Heb 10:24-25). Spiritual disciplines act as rhythms rather than ladders—habits that keep the soul exposed to divine light long enough for photosynthesis of holiness to occur. Vocational faithfulness, hospitality, and justice work spill sanctification outward, ensuring piety does not fossilize into private sentiment. The goal is likeness to Christ integrated into personality so thoroughly that love becomes reflex, not mere resolution. Yet victory, however real, remains partial; aging bodies and systemic evil remind pilgrims that a fuller rescue is scheduled. Sanctification thus awakens longing for the consummating act when the renovation will be unveiled without scaffolding—glorification.

12.1.3 Shall Be Saved Forever: The Awaited Work of Glorification

Glorification is the climactic unveiling of redemption when Christ "will transform our lowly bodies to be like His glorious body" (Phil 3:20-21). In that instant the last vestige of sin's presence evaporates, and mortality is swallowed by life (1 Cor 15:54). The intellect will perceive without distortion, the will will choose without inner sabotage, and affections will blaze with undiluted love for God and neighbor. Resurrection bodies—recognizably ours yet radically renewed—will engage a restored cosmos where art, science, and governance thrive without corruption (Rom 8:21). Justice achieved at the final judgment will silence every accusation, and rewards will individualize grace, displaying the diverse beauty of faithfulness (2 Cor 5:10). The beatific vision will satisfy endless curiosity; seeing God face to face will both complete and perpetually expand joy (1 John 3:2). Relationships purified of envy and suspicion will blossom into community unimaginable in the present age. All work will be worship; cultivating the garden-city will echo Eden while surpassing it in scope and security. This promised future is not escapist fantasy but motivational fuel: knowing destiny arms saints to endure suffering, risk generosity, and labor for justice now (Rom 8:18). Thus glorification closes the arc of salvation yet simultaneously opens eternity's unending chapters of discovery and delight.

With the full panorama—justified once, being sanctified daily, destined for glory—fixed in sight, the task that remains is to translate vision into lifelong worship and resilient mission, themes that the following sections will weave into practical resolve.

12.2 Embodied Response: Living the Integrated Gospel

12.2.1 Whole-Life Worship: Offering Bodies as Living Sacrifices

Paul exhorts believers to present their bodies—a term encompassing mind, emotions, labor, and leisure—as "living sacrifices, holy and acceptable to God," which he calls our "reasonable service" (Rom 12:1). Whole-life worship therefore moves beyond Sunday liturgy, converting kitchens, cubicles, and crosswalks into altars where gratitude is poured out in ordinary actions. Morning routines become doxological when exercise is received as stewardship rather than vanity and breakfast prayers trace ingredients back to the Giver of rain and soil. Commutes morph into mobile sanctuaries; playlists of psalms or silent intercession reorient frazzled nerves before workplace demands. Ethical decisions—filing accurate expense reports, declining gossip invitations—join choral anthems as fragrant offerings that delight the Father as surely as incense did in Solomon's temple. Artistic creativity—coding elegant algorithms, composing jazz riffs, arranging garden beds—celebrates the image of the Creator who fashioned galaxies with a word. Rest, too, is worship when Sabbath naps confess trust in God's providence louder than frantic productivity can. Even bodily limitations become liturgical elements; chronic pain lifted to God with honest lament echoes Christ's own worshipful anguish in Gethsemane. Because every arena is sacred ground, boundaries matter: digital fasting guards attention for communion, and nutritional moderation stewards temples for sustained praise. Children watching parents weave prayer into chores learn that worship is less a compartment than an atmosphere. Corporate services then gather these dispersed sacrifices, offering them in unified thanksgiving that strengthens collective imagination for Monday holiness. As individual altars blaze, sparks leap into relationships, inaugurating the next dimension of embodied response—communal walking.

12.2.2 Communal Walking: Practicing Gospel One-Anothering

The New-Testament vision of church life brims with "one-another" imperatives—love, exhort, forgive, bear burdens—each a relational echo of the Triune fellowship (John 13:34; Gal 6:2). Walking together begins with deliberate presence: small groups that share meals, confessions, and resources cultivate trust deeper than social-media camaraderie. Accountability pairs ask heart-probing questions, turning theoretical repentance into tangible course corrections. Corporate prayer nights transform individual petitions into symphonic intercession, strengthening faith through shared expectancy. Financial koinonia—benevolence funds, micro-loans to entrepreneurs, crowd-funded adoption costs—materializes the claim that kingdom economics overrides scarcity. Conflict, inevitable in proximity, becomes a discipleship laboratory where Matthew 18 reconciliation produces testimonies more persuasive than any sermon. Diversity across ethnicity, generation, and vocation enriches wisdom and exposes blind spots; potluck tables laden with varied cuisines anticipate Revelation's multinational feast (Rev 7:9). Caring for the weak—visiting shut-ins, accommodating special-needs children in worship—signals to a utilitarian society that value is conferred by God, not productivity. Digital channels extend fellowship to diaspora members, yet rhythms of embodied gathering preserve the tactile graces of handshakes and shared Communion cups. Hospitality opens front doors to strangers, converting living rooms into frontlines of evangelism and mutual encouragement. As communal practices mature, the church manifests an apologetic of belonging that beckons outsiders. This magnetic witness propels the third sphere of response—public mission—where internal love overflows into external proclamation.

12.2.3 Public Mission: Bearing Witness in Word and Deed

Jesus commissions His followers as sent ones, promising Spirit-empowered speech that begins in Jerusalem and ripples to the ends of the earth (Acts 1:8). Public mission starts with credible presence—employees who excel, neighbors who serve, students who honor teachers—so that spoken gospel seeds fall on soil already warmed by trust. Evangelism shifts from monologue to dialogue; questions about hope (1 Pet 3:15) receive answers wrapped in humility and narrative rather than combative slogans. Social justice initiatives—anti-trafficking coalitions, prison-mentorship programs, environmental clean-ups—embody the kingdom's ethic, turning abstract love into public policy and neighborhood renewal. Digital spaces host apologetics podcasts and TikTok parables, countering misinformation with creativity and gentleness. Cross-cultural teams learn languages and customs, valuing indigenous leadership to avoid neo-colonial shadows. Marketplace missionaries steward profits for philanthropy, modeling that capitalism can bow to Christ without losing innovative edge. Miraculous interruptions—healings, prophetic insights—still punctuate mission, reminding secular observers that the kingdom is not word only but power (1 Cor 4:20). Persecution, when it arrives, refines testimony; forgiving enemies under media spotlight magnifies the cross more loudly than self-defense ever could. Metrics of success recalibrate from rapid decisions to enduring disciples—communities transformed, injustice decreased, worship established where none existed. As public mission pushes outward, it simultaneously cycles back, enriching personal worship and communal bonds, completing a virtuous loop of embodied response.

Having traced how justified saints worship wholly, walk communally, and witness publicly, we now turn to sustainable rhythms and Spirit-dependence that keep this integrated life vibrant until the day faith becomes sight.

12.3 Sustaining Grace: Rhythms, Reliance, & Readiness

12.3.1 Spirit-Dependence: Breathing in Divine Power for Daily Faithfulness

Christian maturity never graduates from helplessness; it simply learns to convert weakness into continuous dependence on the Spirit who raised Jesus from the dead (Rom 8:11). Dawn prayers of surrender—"fill me afresh"—replace self-talk rooted in grit, reminding the heart that fruit grows only on branches that abide (John 15:5). Throughout the workday, micro-breaths of invocation—"Spirit, guide this e-mail," "Spirit, soften this client meeting"—recalibrate intention before tasks harden into self-reliance. Prompt inner nudges—skip the cynical joke, send the encouragement text—become training drills in real-time obedience. Failure is reinterpreted as feedback: conviction without condemnation ushers saints back to the Spirit's well, where pardon restores communion and wisdom adjusts strategy (1 John 1:9). Communal worship amplifies dependence when congregants voice prophetic encouragements or intercessory burdens, confirming that the church is a living organism animated by one Breath (1 Cor 12:7). Fasting days interrupt routine nourishment to dramatize deeper hunger, clearing static so Spirit whispers grow audible. Even sleep testifies to dependence; turning off screens and relinquishing control entrusts unfinished projects to the One who never slumbers (Ps 121:4). Spiritual gifts blossom in this posture—teaching becomes Spirit-kindled illumination, mercy becomes Spirit-infused empathy—displaying varieties of grace from the same Source (1 Pet 4:10-11). Dependence inoculates against burnout because energy is borrowed, not mustered; the yoke proves easy precisely because power is shared (Matt 11:28-30). Mission gains prophetic edge when strategies emerge

215

from Spirit prompting rather than market analysis alone. Dependence also tempers triumphalism; miraculous breakthroughs prompt worship, not ego inflation, for everyone remembers whose wind filled the sails. By cultivating reflexive reliance, believers keep justification's assurance from morphing into presumption and sanctification's effort from curdling into legalism. This life-breath of the Spirit now grounds the practical scaffolding of sustainable rhythms.

12.3.2 Rhythms of Renewal: Crafting Rules of Life that Endure Seasons

Because disciples inhabit twenty-four-hour bodies, grace embeds itself in patterns that sync soul with calendar (Ps 90:12). Crafting a rule of life starts with inventory: noting energy peaks, relational callings, and weak points where temptation prowls. Daily anchors—scripture meditation with first coffee, midday examen walk, evening gratitude review—bookend activities with divine awareness. Weekly cadences layer on: communal worship, technology sabbath, family game night, and meal prep that frames food as fellowship rather than fuel. Monthly rhythms include half-day solitude retreats or creativity blocs—painting, woodwork, poetry—where play thickens joy. Quarterly rhythms might feature financial generosity reviews, ensuring money remains servant not master (Matt 6:24). Annual checkpoints—silent retreats, intercultural mission trips—offer panoramic reflection, adjusting the rule for new seasons: newborns, empty nests, career shifts. Crucially, the rule guards margins; white space on the calendar signals faith that God—not hustle—secures future provision. Flexibility is baked in: illness loosens schedule rigidity, and Spirit promptings sometimes override planned productivity for spontaneous compassion. Community feedback keeps the rule honest; mentors flag perfectionistic bloat or hidden avoidance disguised as rest. Digital dashboards or paper planners visualize habits, transforming abstract intention into trackable reality. Over years, these grooves carve neurological pathways where virtue flows with less friction, liberating cognitive bandwidth for creativity and service. As rhythms mature, they act like ballast during storms—grief or relocation jostles external order, but inner liturgy steadies devotion. Yet vigilance remains necessary; long obedience can drift into autopilot, so the final subsection addresses watchful readiness that keeps rhythms alive with anticipation.

12.3.3 Watchful Readiness: Practicing Joyful Alertness for the Lord's Return

Jesus' parables of the vigilant servant and trimmed-lamp virgins warn disciples that complacency, not persecution, most often dulls expectancy (Luke 12:35-40; Matt 25:1-13). Watchfulness begins with eschatological literacy— understanding that signs of the times include both global convulsions and ordinary apathy (2 Tim 3:1-5). Calendars reflect expectancy through built-in pauses for prophetic contemplation: Advent fasts that ache for light, resurrection-season generosity sprees that echo empty-tomb abundance. Families keep "second-coming journals," recording world events alongside prayers, teaching children to interpret headlines through gospel lenses rather than fear cycles. Gratitude lists become acts of resistance, refusing cynicism's narrative that nothing changes until heaven; each answered prayer is a rehearsal for cosmic restoration. Hospitality doubles as readiness training; hosting strangers may entertain angels and certainly trains hearts for the marriage supper (Heb 13:2). Spiritual warfare drills—regular armor meditations, communal confession of besetting sins—maintain combat readiness against lukewarm drift (Eph 6:10-18). Watchful communities budget for benevolence spikes during crises, viewing economic downturns as evangelistic windows rather than apocalyptic doom. Artistic expressions—mural projects depicting New Jerusalem skylines—plant visual reminders across urban landscapes that history has a destination. Even funeral liturgies preach readiness, framing death not as final curtain but as dress rehearsal for resurrection morning. Daily benedictions conclude with "Come, Lord Jesus," so the last word before dispersal engraves hope on departing minds (Rev 22:20). Such practices keep hearts limber, ensuring that when the sky finally rends, saints lift heads in recognition, not terror.

Transition to Section 12.4 Spirit-dependence, sustainable rhythms, and vigilant hope together sustain believers on the long road from justification's gate to glorification's horizon, preparing us for a concluding summons to lifelong doxology and unwavering trust in the God who carries us every step.

Conclusion

Salvation is a journey with a reliable Guide, a present Companion, and a certain destination. Looking back, gratitude swells for the cross where guilt was canceled; looking around, courage rises for the Spirit who supplies strength; looking ahead, joy ignites for the day when faith will become sight. To embrace that whole journey is to live every ordinary hour as a foretaste of an extraordinary future, to wield every gift for the good of neighbor and the honor of Christ, and to rest each night in the Father's unrelenting faithfulness. May the vision rehearsed in these chapters convert into prayer on our lips, endurance in our steps, and praise in our communities—until the trumpet sounds and the three-tense gospel resolves in everlasting, all-surpassing glory.

www.ingramcontent.com/pod-product-compliance
Lightning Source LLC
Chambersburg PA
CBHW060317050426
42449CB00011B/2526